Final Assembly and Checkout Alternatives

for the Joint Strike Fighter

Cynthia R. Cook

Mark V. Arena

John C. Graser

John A. Ausink

Lloyd S. Dixon

Timothy E. Liston

Sheila E. Murray

Susan A. Resetar

Chad Shirley

Jerry Sollinger

Obaid Younossi

Prepared for the
National Defense Research Institute

Approved for public release; distribution unlimited

RAND

National Defense Research Institute

The research described in this report was sponsored by the Office of the Secretary of Defense (OSD). The research was conducted in RAND's National Defense Research Institute, a federally funded research and development center supported by the OSD, the Joint Staff, the unified commands, and the defense agencies under Contract DASW01-01-C-0004.

Library of Congress Cataloging-in-Publication Data

Final assembly and checkout alternatives for the joint strike fighter / Cynthia R. Cook
... [et al.].
    p. cm.
    "MR-1559."
    Includes bibliographical references.
    ISBN 0-8330-3210-0
    1. X-32 (Jet fighter plane) 2. X-35 (Jet fighter plane) 3. United States—Armed
Forces—Procurement. I. Cook, Cynthia R., 1965–

UG1242.F5 F538 2002
623.7'464'0973—dc21

                                 2002026567

Cover photographs by Lockheed Martin

RAND is a nonprofit institution that helps improve policy and decisionmaking through research and analysis. RAND® is a registered trademark. RAND's publications do not necessarily reflect the opinions or policies of its research sponsors.

Cover design by Stephen Bloodsworth

Published 2002 by RAND
1700 Main Street, P.O. Box 2138, Santa Monica, CA 90407-2138
1200 South Hayes Street, Arlington, VA 22202-5050
201 North Craig Street, Suite 202, Pittsburgh, PA 15213-1516
RAND URL: http://www.rand.org/
To order RAND documents or to obtain additional information,
contact Distribution Services: Telephone: (310) 451-7002;
Fax: (310) 451-6915; Email: order@rand.org

PREFACE

This report responds to a congressional request to examine the implications of alternative strategies for performing the final assembly and checkout of the Joint Strike Fighter. The task includes identifying reasonable alternative facilities and determining the cost of doing all or part of the work at these locations. Currently, the primary contractor, Lockheed Martin, plans to perform these operations at its plant in Fort Worth, Texas. This research was sponsored by the Office of the Under Secretary of Defense for Acquisition, Technology, and Logistics and the Joint Strike Fighter Program Office. It should be of interest to those involved with the procurement of military weapon systems, particularly those involved with or interested in fighter aircraft.

The work was conducted for the Office of the Secretary of Defense within the Acquisition and Technology Policy Center of RAND's National Defense Research Institute, a federally funded research and development center sponsored by the Office of the Secretary of Defense, the Joint Staff, the unified commands, and the defense agencies.

CONTENTS

Preface   iii

Figures   xi

Tables   xiii

Summary   xv

Acknowledgments   xxi

Abbreviations   xxiii

Chapter One
   INTRODUCTION   1
   History of the Joint Strike Fighter   1
      JSF Competition   2
   Origins of This Study   4
   Final Assembly and Checkout of the
       Joint Strike Fighter   5
   Purpose of the Study   10
      FACO Strategies   10
      Methodology   12
   How This Report Is Organized   13

Chapter Two
   SPLITTING PRODUCTION   15
   Introduction   15
   General Policy Issues Related to Splitting Defense
       Production   15
   JSF   19
   Arguments For and Against Splitting Production   21

Contractor Performance 21
Industrial Base............................... 23
Avoidance of Risk 25
Capacity 25
Strategic Buffer 26
Share Economic Benefit 27
The U.S. Experience 29
Three Post–World War II Aircraft: F-86,
F-100, and B-52 29
Coproduction of an Aircraft 31
The European Experience 32
Coproduction of Navy Systems by
Multiple Contractors 33
Conclusion 36

Chapter Three
SITE SELECTION ISSUES: PLANT AND MAJOR FACILITY
REQUIREMENTS FOR FACO 37
Specific Site Physical Requirements 38
Categories of FACO Options 38
Option 1: A "Greenfield" Site 39
Option 2: A Site with an Existing Airfield Only 41
Option 3: An Airfield with Existing Buildings Capable of
Supporting JSF FACO 42
Option 4: A Site with a Current DoD Operation or
Depot Activity with Excess Building Capacity 43
Option 5: Selecting a Site with a Current Military
Aircraft Production Line That Has Sufficient Capacity
to Accommodate JSF FACO Operations 44
Option and Sites Chosen for Analysis 45
Conclusion 48

Chapter Four
JSF WORKFORCE ISSUES 49
Workforce Issues............................. 49
Labor 49
Labor Skills for the JSF......................... 50
Task Distribution and Total Workforce Size
for FACO 51
Standard Occupational Classification System 52
Cost of Labor................................. 53

Other Costs Related to the Workforce   54
   Training and Other Costs Related to Special
      Requirements   54
   Workers' Compensation Costs   55
   Special Costs Related to Different Locations   56
   Costs Related to Mandated Benefits for Employees   56
   Hiring and Training Incentive Programs   57
Availability of Workers   58
Summary   59

Chapter Five
INDIRECT COSTS   61
Background   61
Effect of Indirect Costs on JSF FACO Location   65

Chapter Six
STATE AND LOCAL TAX CREDITS AND INCENTIVES . . .   67
State and Local Economic Development   73
   Effectiveness of Development Programs   73
State and Local Taxes in California, Georgia, and Texas . .   74
   State Franchise and Corporate Income Taxes   75
   Property Taxes   75
   Sales and Use Taxes   76
Tax Credits and Deductions   77
   State and Local Economic Development Programs   77
   Texas   77
   Georgia   78
   California   79
Summary   82

Chapter Seven
ENVIRONMENTAL COSTS   83
Emissions Sources   84
   Air Emissions   84
   Noise   86
   Other Environmental Issues   86
Environmental Compliance Costing Approach   88
   Background   88
   Environment Cost Estimating Overview   89
Compliance Costs for Air Emissions   92
   Fort Worth   97
   Marietta   97

Lockheed Martin–Palmdale   99
Northrop Grumman–Palmdale   101
Intangible Environmental Issues   102
Community Activism   102
Regulatory Atmosphere   103
Enforcement Aggressiveness   105
Summary   105

Chapter Eight
OTHER COST FACTORS: STEALTH, SUPPLIERS,
AND ENERGY   107
JSF Stealth.   107
An Overview of the JSF Stealth Requirements   107
JSF Airframe Stealth Approach During the
Manufacturing Process   109
Costs of Stealth for JSF FACO   111
The Supplier and Technical Support Base, Suppliers, and
Transportation Costs   112
Supplier and Technical Support Base   112
Supplier Representation on Site   115
Logistics and Transportation Costs   115
Summary of Supplier Issues   117
Energy   118
The Cost of Electricity   119
Reliability   122

Chapter Nine
MODELING THE COST IMPLICATIONS OF
ALTERNATIVE FACO STRATEGIES FOR JSF
PRODUCTION   125
Cost Elements in the Model   126
Production Labor   126
Indirect Costs   132
Investments: Facilities, Equipment, and Tooling   135
Taxes and Incentives   137
Environmental and Permitting Costs   141
Transportation   141
Power   143
Management and Supplier Support   144
Fee   144

Model Structure   145
   Interaction Among Cost Elements   145
   FACO Production Strategy Assumptions   146
Conclusion   147

Chapter Ten
RESULTS   149
Introduction   149
Cost to Whom?   149
FACO Alternatives   152
   Impact of FACO Activities on Site Workload   154
   Base Case Versus Alternatives   155
   Sensitivity Analysis   157
Conclusion   163

Chapter Eleven
CONCLUSIONS.   165
Cost   165
Other Policy Arguments   166
Summary   167

Appendix
A. LEGISLATIVE LANGUAGE: THE FLOYD D. SPENCE
    NATIONAL DEFENSE AUTHORIZATION ACT FOR
    FISCAL YEAR 2001   169

B. JSF FACO SITE ASSESSMENT   171

C. WAGE COMPARISONS   183

D. ENVIRONMENTAL REGULATORY PROCESS   185

Bibliography   193

FIGURES

1.1.   Lockheed Martin JSF Design   3
1.2.   Final Assembly and Checkout   6
2.1.   Continuum of Procurement Production
       Alternatives   17
2.2.   Fighter Aircraft Production Schedules   23
2.3.   States with Significant Involvement in JSF
       Production   28
9.1.   Relationships Between FACO Cost Elements   145
9.2.   Example Time Line for FACO Production   148
10.1. FACO Workload Share for Alternatives 1–4   154
10.2. Total Additional Fixed Indirect Costs of FACO
       Activities   160
10.3. Cost Sensitivity to Change in Start Year of Multisite
       FACO for Alternative 5   160
10.4. Cost Sensitivity to Change in Start Year of Multisite
       FACO for Alternative 7   161
10.5. Sensitivity to Different Learning Transfer Fractions of
       Alternative 5   162

TABLES

S.1.	FACO Strategies Considered	xvi
S.2.	FACO Option Cost Comparisons	xvii
1.1.	JSF Aircraft Costs by Variant	4
1.2.	Cycle Time Required for FACO Activities	9
2.1.	Skills Maintained by Range of Production Alternatives	20
3.1.	Facilities Requirements for JSF FACO	47
4.1.	Touch Labor Skill Distribution for F-16 Mate-Through-Delivery	51
4.2.	Standard Hourly Breakdown for JSF (CTOL Version)	52
4.3.	FACO Activities and Associated SOC Codes	53
6.1.	State Taxes and Their Impact on JSF FACO	68
6.2.	California Tax Credits and Incentives	70
6.3.	Georgia Tax Credits and Incentives	72
7.1.	Total Annual Air Emissions Estimates for a Maximum Production Rate of 17 Aircraft per Month	85
7.2	Facilities and Equipment Required to Control Air Emissions	93
7.3.	Environmental Analyses and Permitting Costs	95
7.4.	Summary of Air Emissions and Control Costs	96
8.1.	Comparison of the Stealth Implementation in the Legacy System to the JSF Approach	110
8.2.	FACO Suppliers	113
8.3.	Electric Power Industry Generation by Energy Source, 1999	119
9.1.	Investments Required for FACO (Contractor-Owned)	138

9.2.   Investments Required for FACO (Government-
        Owned)   138
10.1.   Cost Differences for Various FACO Alternatives   156
10.2.   Contributions to Relative Costs—JSF FACO
        Perspective   158
10.3.   Contributions to Relative Costs—DoD Perspective . . .   159
10.4.   Relative Cost Increases for Various FACO
        Alternatives—Discounted at 3.5 Percent
        per Annum   163
C.1.   Wage Comparisons   183

BACKGROUND AND OBJECTIVE

In October 2001, the Department of Defense (DoD) awarded a contract for System Development and Demonstration (SDD) of the Joint Strike Fighter (JSF) to the Lockheed Martin Aeronautics Company. The JSF program, which is expected to run for more than two decades and cost $300 billion,[1] will deliver 3,002 fighter/attack aircraft to the U.S. Air Force, Navy, and Marine Corps, as well as to the UK Ministry of Defence. The JSF will replace U.S. Air Force F-16s and A-10s and complement the F-22; complement carrier-based U.S. Navy F/A-18E/Fs; replace U.S. Marine Corps AV-8Bs and F/A-18C/Ds; and replace UK Harrier aircraft.

The primary reason for developing a single aircraft with three variants to fulfill the missions of the different services was to minimize cost. The result of having a single program will be considerable commonality among the three variants (conventional takeoff and landing [CTOL], carrier variant [CV], and short takeoff/vertical landing [STOVL]). This commonality will reduce both initial procurement and ongoing life-cycle costs, relative to having three unrelated aircraft.

Many companies spread across the United States and the world will be building the various components and subassemblies of the JSF. Lockheed Martin plans to assemble the major components of the JSF

---

[1] Then-year dollars.

and test the aircraft at its Fort Worth, Texas, plant, in a process called final assembly and checkout, or FACO. The U.S. Congress has directed DoD to examine alternatives to the single-site FACO plan. This examination is to include a determination of potential locations for FACO and an analysis of the implications of carrying out the process at multiple locations. DoD asked RAND's National Defense Research Institute to carry out the study. This report describes the methodology and results of that study.

WHAT WE FOUND

Although the legislation was quite clear about examining the implications of spreading the FACO work across multiple sites, it did not specify precisely how that should be done. Multiple options exist. All aircraft variants could be assembled at one site or another, different variants could be assembled at each site, or there could be some combination. Four sites were analyzed in this study, including the Lockheed Martin plants at Fort Worth; Marietta, Ga.; and Palmdale, Calif., and a Northrop Grumman plant, also at Palmdale. We considered the nine options shown in Table S.1, comparing the cost of each against the baseline of having Fort Worth conduct FACO for all JSF aircraft. These options do not represent all possible approaches, of

Table S.1

FACO Strategies Considered

Alternative	Description
1	100% of FACO at Lockheed Martin–Fort Worth (Baseline)
2	100% of FACO at Lockheed Martin–Palmdale
3	100% of FACO at Lockheed Martin–Marietta
4	100% of FACO at Northrop Grumman–Palmdale
5	50% of FACO at Lockheed Martin–Fort Worth, and 50% at Lockheed Martin–Palmdale
6	50% of FACO at Lockheed Martin–Fort Worth, and 50% at Northrop Grumman–Palmdale
7	50% FACO at Lockheed Martin–Fort Worth, and 50% at Lockheed Martin–Marietta
8	All CTOL at Lockheed Martin–Fort Worth, and all CV and STOVL at Lockheed Martin–Marietta
9	One-third of all production at each of the Lockheed Martin sites

course, but represent a reasonable sample of the potential alternatives.

In our analysis of the alternatives, we found no efficiency, effectiveness, or cost reasons to split FACO operations between two sites or across multiple sites.

Moving some or all JSF FACO from Fort Worth to another location would result in additional costs to DoD. Table S.2 compares the costs of the alternatives listed in Table S.1. The numbers in Table S.2 represent the differences in cost from the baseline case of doing all the work in Fort Worth (in 2002 dollars). Because sites have more than one defense program and because the effects among programs interact, we show two sets of comparative costs. One includes only the effects on JSF FACO; the other includes the effects on all DoD programs at all affected sites. The second column represents the costs to DoD as a whole and better portrays the overall budget implications of various FACO strategies.

All the alternatives that divide the work across one or more additional sites increase costs, due to loss of learning and duplicate facilities and tooling. Furthermore, moving FACO activity from Fort

Table S.2

FACO Option Cost Comparisons (millions FY02$)

Alternative	JSF FACO Costs	DoD Costs[a]
1	0.0	0.0
2	4.0	256.9
3	132.1	74.1
4	199.0	656.7
5	310.3	221.5
6	328.4	386.4
7	331.8	117.1
8	419.1	134.7
9	501.7	277.6

[a]Includes cost effects from JSF FACO.
NOTE: For description of alternatives, see Table S.1 on the previous page.

Worth changes the overall DoD costs because of the effect on indirect costs for other DoD work. The costs of the rest of the JSF work under way at that plant, as well as of the other programs there, will increase because these programs will have to bear a greater fraction of the Fort Worth overhead costs. This indirect cost increase is not offset by a corresponding decrease for programs at the alternative FACO sites.

Cost differences from the baseline strategy are actually a combination of many potential factors, such as effects on overhead rates, inefficiencies in splitting production from loss of learning, additional investments that the baseline site may not require (because of SDD facilities and tooling being in place at Fort Worth), differing manufacturing costs (e.g., rates for labor, power, management, taxes), stricter environmental regulations, and additional management and oversight effort required to manage an additional manufacturing location that is not required for the baseline facility. It should also be noted that even the most expensive alternative adds less than 10 percent to the cost of FACO, which is only two percent of the total JSF unit recurring flyaway cost.

We assessed some reasons for splitting FACO that might reflect benefits not included in our cost analysis and discuss them below. These included inducing competition among alternate sites, avoiding capacity constraints, maintaining the military aircraft industrial base, maintaining excess capacity for surge or as insurance against natural or man-made disasters, and extending the local economic benefits associated with FACO to more than one region. We did not find any of these to be compelling enough to split JSF FACO.

At the contract award, DoD reaffirmed that the JSF will be a "winner take all" program. Thus, it has already decided not to induce competition among different potential manufacturers in the production phase.

Another reason for splitting FACO might be that a single site lacks the capacity to produce on the desired schedule. Lockheed Martin's analysis indicates that Fort Worth can deliver the required number of aircraft on schedule and, therefore, there appears to be no capacity argument for opening another FACO site.

Some might argue that establishing another FACO site would help maintain a more robust industrial base. However, our analysis indicates that design and overall aircraft program management are the most complex tasks in military aircraft acquisition and the ones for which maintaining a robust industrial base is likely most critical. These tasks are not under study here. Maintaining the capability to do the tasks involved in final assembly and checkout is less at risk because it is maintained by other manned and unmanned aircraft in production and, to a certain extent, by normal maintenance activities. Thus, multiple FACO sites do not appear to be critical to the industrial base.

The arguments for having multiple sites that focus on the maintenance of extra capacity as a buffer against possible future production surges—or in case of natural or man-made disasters at one or another location—also do not provide compelling arguments in favor of splitting FACO.

Arguably, a case could be made to extend FACO operations to more than one site so that a broader segment of the population would reap the economic benefits of the project. Although FACO operations represent a relatively small portion of the overall contract award, even a modest segment of a $300 billion program could amount to significant economic activity over the life of the contract. We offer three observations in this regard. First, the locales where FACO operations are feasible are not economically depressed. The unemployment rate at each is either less than the national average or about the same. Second, the number of new jobs created by FACO operations is not very large in terms of a regional workforce. FACO involves about 1,200 workers and, thus, the net gain in total employment in any given area would be relatively modest. Third, the rationale underpinning the JSF contract—a single development and production program producing three variants with many common characteristics—was to allow DoD to procure the aircraft at the lowest possible cost. Splitting FACO may provide economic benefit to some limited locality, but the costs must be borne by all taxpayers. Splitting FACO operations seems to be at odds with this rationale, as well as with the spirit of acquisition reform, which calls for a reduction in the amount of unnecessary government oversight and control of the specifics of military procurements.

This work could not have been undertaken without the special relationship that exists between the Office of the Secretary of Defense (OSD) and RAND under the National Defense Research Institute (NDRI). For that relationship we are grateful. Many individuals at OSD, Lockheed Martin, Northrop Grumman, RAND, and those at many other organizations deserve credit for the work discussed in this report. Their names and contributions would fill several pages.

Ron Mutzelburg, Deputy Director of Air Warfare in the Office of the Under Secretary of Defense for Acquisition, Technology, and Logistics, and Michael Novak provided useful support and oversight throughout the course of the project.

This work was kicked off when MGen. Michael Hough was Program Director of the Joint Strike Fighter. At that time, Col Darrell H. Holcomb served as our point of contact in the program office. We are grateful for their support at the beginning of this research effort. As we finished our research, Program Director Maj Gen John L. Hudson and Col Tony Romano provided leadership and insights. Several cost analysts in the program office, including Lt Col Grant McVicker and Jennifer Sawyer, also provided critical assistance.

Jack Keashon of the Defense Contract Management Agency (DCMA) in Philadelphia provided significant assistance in developing and organizing the administration of the DCMA survey of the potential FACO sites. Without his help, this research would have been less completely realized. We also would like to thank Marjorie Heilweil for help in survey development, and the on-site contract management officers for collecting the data.

CAPT David Lewis furnished insight into the multisite production of ships and submarines for the U.S. Navy, as well as contacts for further interviews.

Many people from the contractors involved provided assistance as well. Larry McQuien of Lockheed Martin in Fort Worth and many others at Lockheed Martin were willing to answer what must have seemed like an endless stream of questions on the many different issues covered in this report. Without their help, this research would not have been possible. George Legg of Northrop Grumman also assisted the research effort by providing data and insights.

At RAND, Christopher Horn provided research assistance, and Michele Anandappa provided both research assistance and administrative support. The skillful editing of Daniel Sheehan and Phillip Wirtz improved the readability of this report.

We particularly wish to thank our RAND colleagues Michael Kennedy and Frank Lacroix. Their careful and thoughtful reviews strengthened this research significantly.

ABBREVIATIONS

AEO	Annual Energy Outlook
AFMC	Air Force Materiel Command
AFP	Air Force Plant
ANG	Air National Guard
AVAQMD	Antelope Valley Air Quality Management District
AVEZ	Antelope Valley Enterprise Zone
BACT	Best Available Control Technology
BLS	Bureau of Labor Statistics
CAAA	Clean Air Act Amendments
CAD/CAM	Computer-aided design/computer-aided manufacturing
CAIG	Cost Analysis Improvement Group
CDP	Concept Demonstration Phase
CEQA	California Environmental Quality Act
CER	Cost-estimating relationship
CEV	Civil Engineering, Environment Division
CO	Carbon monoxide
COM	Cost of money

CONUS	Continental United States
CTOL	Conventional takeoff and landing
CV	Carrier variant
DARPA	Defense Advanced Research Projects Agency
DCMA	Defense Contract Management Agency
DoD	U.S. Department of Defense
DSMC	Defense Systems Management College
EA	Environmental Assessment
ESH	Environmental Safety and Health
EIA	Energy Information Administration
EIS	Environmental Impact Statement
EMS	Environmental management system
EO/IR	Electro-optical/infrared
EPA	U.S. Environmental Protection Agency
FAA	Federal Aviation Administration
FACO	Final assembly and checkout
FCF	Functional Check Flight
FPRA	Forward Pricing Rate Agreement
FRP	Full-rate production
FTE	Full-time equivalent (employees)
FY	Fiscal year
G&A	General and administrative
HAP	Hazardous air pollutant
HVAC	Heating, ventilation, and air conditioning
I&E	Installations and Environment
ILE	Installations, logistics, and environment
ISO	International Standards Organization

IWTA	Intercompany Work Transfer Agreement
JPO	Joint Program Office
JSF	Joint Strike Fighter
kWh	Kilowatt hour
LRIP	Low-rate initial production
MIC	Manufacturing Investment Credit
MOD	Ministry of Defence (United Kingdom)
MSA	Metropolitan statistical area
NAAQS	National Ambient Air Quality Standards
NEMS	National Energy Modeling System
NEPA	National Environmental Policy Act
NESHAP	National Emissions Standards for Hazardous Air Pollutants
NOx	Nitrogen oxides
NPV	Net present value
NSR	New Source Review
OES	Occupational Employment Statistics
OSD	Office of the Secretary of Defense
OSHA	Occupational Safety and Health Administration
PESHE	Programmatic environmental, safety, and health evaluation
PM	Particulate matter
PTMS	Power thermal management system
RAM	Radar-absorbing material
RAS	Radar-absorbing structure
RCS	Radar cross section
SDD	System Development and Demonstration

SOC	Standard Occupational Classification
STOVL	Short takeoff/vertical landing
UK	United Kingdom
URF	Unit recurring flyaway
USAF	U.S. Air Force
USMC	U.S. Marine Corps
USN	U.S. Navy
VOC	Volatile organic compound
WBS	Work breakdown structure

Chapter One

INTRODUCTION

This report assesses the cost and policy implications of conducting Joint Strike Fighter (JSF) final assembly and checkout (FACO) at different potential locations and with different work splits, rather than doing all the work at a single location—which is Lockheed Martin's current plan. The study was mandated by the U.S. Congress in the FY 2001 Appropriations Bill.[1]

HISTORY OF THE JOINT STRIKE FIGHTER

The JSF emerged from technology and aircraft development efforts in the early 1990s as a joint aircraft designed to meet the long-term air-to-surface needs of the three services that operate strike aircraft. It originated from several advanced aircraft programs, including the Navy's Advanced Attack/Fighter (A/F-X) meant to replace the canceled A-12 and a Defense Advanced Research Projects Agency (DARPA) project examining an advanced short takeoff and vertical landing capability. The JSF was designed to

- Replace U.S. Air Force F-16s and A-10s, and complement the F-22

- Augment carrier-based U.S. Navy F/A-18E/Fs

- Replace U.S. Marine Corps AV-8Bs and F/A-18 C/Ds

- Replace UK Harrier aircraft.

---

[1] Floyd D. Spence National Defense Authorization Act for Fiscal Year 2001; exact language can be found in Appendix A.

JSF Competition

The U.S. Department of Defense (DoD) Bottom-Up Review of 1993 made certain recommendations for aviation, including "continue the ongoing F-22 and F/A-18E/F programs, cancel the Multirole Fighter and the A/F-X programs, curtail F-16 and F/A-18C/D procurement and initiate the JAST Program."[2] (JAST, or Joint Advanced Strike Technology, was the name of the JSF's predecessor.) This was done to create building blocks for affordable development of the next-generation strike fighter. Within the next year, more work was consolidated into the effort; "the JAST program had absorbed the DARPA Common Affordable Lightweight Fighter (CALF) program."[3]

In December 1994, four companies—Boeing, Lockheed Martin, McDonnell Douglas, and Northrop Grumman—were awarded 15-month Concept Definition and Design Research contracts. Northrop Grumman and McDonnell Douglas/British Aerospace then agreed to work together. After various program reviews, Boeing and Lockheed Martin won Concept Demonstration Phase (CDP) prime contracts in November 1996. Boeing then merged with McDonnell Douglas, while Lockheed Martin began working with Northrop Grumman and British Aerospace (later, BAE Systems). By this time, the program had been renamed the JSF.

After five years of the CDP, on October 26, 2001, DoD awarded the System Development and Demonstration (SDD) contract of almost $19 billion to Lockheed Martin, as the final step in the winner-take-all competition.[4]

According to current plans, low-rate initial production (LRIP) is scheduled to begin in 2006. Full-rate production (FRP) of 206 aircraft per year will begin in 2012. The last U.S. aircraft will be ordered in 2026.

When completed, the JSF program will be one of the largest aircraft acquisition programs in U.S. history, worth some $300 billion (then-year dollars) over the next quarter-century. A total of 3,002 aircraft in

---

[2]http://www.jsf.mil.

[3]http://www.jsf.mil.

[4]A description of the announcement can be found at http://www.defenselink.mil/news/Oct2001/b10262001_bt543-01.html (last accessed May 30, 2002).

three configurations—a conventional takeoff and landing (CTOL) variant, a short takeoff/vertical landing (STOVL) variant, and a carrier variant (CV)—will be produced for DoD and for the UK Ministry of Defence (MOD). Figure 1.1 portrays the three variants of Lockheed Martin's proposal aircraft.[5]

Current acquisition plans call for the U.S. Air Force to buy 1,763 CTOL aircraft. The U.S. Navy will buy 480 of the CV aircraft, and the U.S. Marine Corps will purchase 609 STOVL aircraft. The MOD will procure 150 aircraft, most likely of the STOVL variety. It is estimated that other foreign customers could purchase an additional 3,000 aircraft. Indeed, a number of countries have already committed to participating in the program.

From the outset, affordability has been an important goal of the JSF program. In 1994, DoD established target prices for each variant. Table 1 presents these targets along with their value in FY 2002 dollars, which is the baseline used in this report.

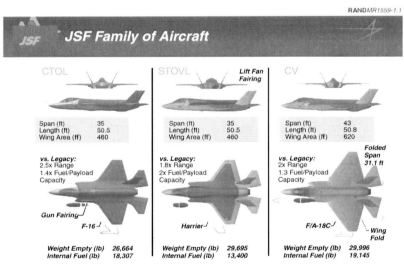

Figure 1.1—Lockheed Martin JSF Design

---

[5]The design shown represents the proposal version of the JSF and does not necessarily reflect the final aircraft configuration.

Table 1.1

JSF Aircraft Costs by Variant (millions $)

Variant	Original Program Goals	
	FY 1994	FY 2002
CTOL	28.0	31.6
STOVL	30.0–35.0	33.8–39.5
CV	31.0–38.0	35.0–42.8

ORIGINS OF THIS STUDY

Lockheed Martin's current plan for the JSF is to perform all FACO work at its Fort Worth, Texas. plant. Congress has directed DoD to examine alternatives, including determining the different potential locations for JSF FACO and the implications of conducting JSF FACO at multiple locations, and to report on this within 180 days of contract award. The provisions of the FY 2001 Defense Authorization Act (see Appendix A), which mandated the study, stipulated that it accomplish the following:

• Examine JSF FACO at one, two, and multiple locations.

• Identify the potential locations for FACO.

• Estimate the costs of assembly and checkout at each location based on a reasonable annual procurement estimate.

• Compare costs across locations.

In carrying out these comparisons, the legislation directed the study to consider the following elements:

• State tax credits.

• State and local incentives.

• Skilled resident workforce.

• Supplier and technical support bases.

• Available stealth production facilities.

• Environmental standards.

RAND identified a number of other elements that differ among sites and included them in the cost analysis as well. These include indirect costs, taxes, transportation, and energy.

FINAL ASSEMBLY AND CHECKOUT OF THE JOINT STRIKE FIGHTER

As the name of the process implies, final assembly and checkout involves workers assembling major components and "checking out" the aircraft system performance. The process, which Lockheed Martin also calls "mate through delivery," includes four major activities: structural mate, tail installation and systems mate, final assembly, and systems checkout and tests. Figure 1.2 shows the assembly process.

Structural mate joins the four primary aircraft components (the three portions of the fuselage to the wing) and includes the installation of the main landing gear. First, the wing is attached to the center fuselage, then the aft fuselage to the center fuselage, and finally the forward fuselage to the center fuselage. These aircraft components already contain most of the electronics and hydraulic subsystems. Edges may or may not be installed on the wing before final assembly. During tail installation/subsystems mate, the remaining aircraft systems are installed, and the vertical tails and horizontal stabilizers and the main landing gear access doors are also installed. The electrical, hydraulic, fuel, etc., systems are connected across the mate joints. Necessary checks are made to ensure proper function and connections. Other miscellaneous systems and structural parts are also installed.

Final assembly and final systems test involves installation and test of the cockpit seat, canopy, propulsion system, engine bay doors, weapons bay doors, radome, high-dollar components,[6] and gun (CTOL variant only). All systems are to be checked out using either built-in-test or special test equipment. Final assembly and testing is complete at this point.

---

[6]Lockheed Martin plans to install certain expensive components, such as the lift fan, engine, and radar, during final assembly operations to save a few weeks of inventory costs on those items.

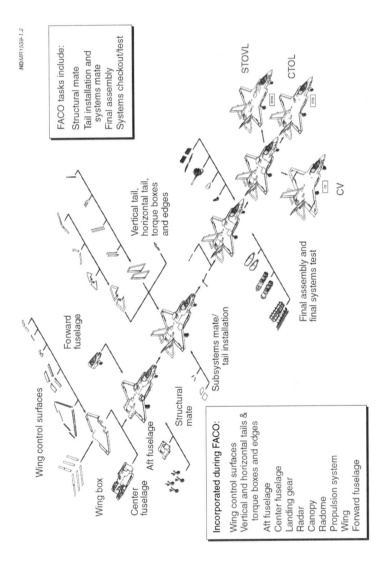

SOURCE: Lockheed Martin Aeronautics Company.

Figure 1.2—Final Assembly and Checkout

Final finish and verification work during FACO is not extensive because most of the paint and special coatings are applied at the module level. Remaining areas of the aircraft will be robotically coated. To verify the low-observable characteristics of the aircraft, it will be mounted on a turntable and its signature will be tested. In the fuel racks barn, the aircraft is fueled for the first time, any leaks are identified and repaired, and the fuel system is calibrated.

Finally, field operations include testing of certain components and performing a number of operations:

- fuel/wet system test indicators.

- engine feed checkout.

- fuselage transfer tank.

- fuel/wet systems test transfer.

- fuel level sense.

- remote input/outputs—fuel, hydraulics.

- fuel/ground refuel receptacle.

- fuel/aerial refuel receptacle fuel function.

- OBIGGS (on-board inert gas-generating system).

- escape system checkout.

- survival kit/seawars system checkout.

- green engine run (auxiliary power unit, environmental control systems, engine).

- engine starter/general checkout.

- bleed air/emergency power mode, integrated power package checkout.

- Environmental Control System ground test.

- cabin pressure checkout.

- on-board oxygen-generating system checkout.

- green engine run (preflight and mechanical).

- CSFDR (crash survivable functional data recorder) download/clear.
- prognostic health management checkout.
- flight readiness checkout.
- company FCF[7] number 1.
- company FCF number 2.
- DD-250.[8]

The JSF will be the first fighter program that attempts to satisfy the needs of three different services using three highly common variants of a single design. The DoD program goal has been that each variant would have high commonality with the other two variants, on the order of 70–90 percent. This commonality is depicted in Figure 1.1. In theory, such commonality should make the JSF more affordable during production and throughout the service life of the aircraft. Because FACO activities for each variant of the JSF are highly common, it is reasonable to build the multiple variants on a single production line. Lockheed Martin has indicated that this would be its plan unless directed to do otherwise.

The total direct labor hours required for these tasks are divided into the categories of fuselage structural mate, subsystems mate, final assembly/test, flight operations, manloads/ITLs,[9] and final finishes. Total support labor required for FACO is divided into the categories of manufacturing engineering, tool engineering, tool manufacturing, quality control, engineering, and material inventory. (Note that these categories are specific to Lockheed Martin.)

The JSF takes advantage of recent advances in aircraft design tools and concepts, which should improve the quality and shorten the cycle time for the required FACO processes. These include advances in tooling concepts and improvements in computer-aided design/computer-aided manufacturing (CAD/CAM) including three-

---

[7]Functional Check Flight.

[8]Delivery to the customer.

[9]ITLs are incomplete task logs. This category refers to the labor that must be done to delivered subassemblies to ready them for FACO.

dimensional solids modeling tools. The JSF design incorporates very few attachment points compared with legacy systems. The airframe mate of the major subassemblies will be accomplished through a numerically controlled laser alignment system. Electrical and hydraulic systems are joined using adapter plates. Given these technologies, which facilitate the assembly process and reduce the need for complex assembly tools, jigs, and fixtures, Lockheed Martin's total expected time for mate through delivery is 40.8 workdays. The time can be broken out as shown in Table 1.2.

By way of comparison, Lockheed Martin's planned FACO cycle time for the 257th JSF aircraft is expected to be half that of the F-16, a much less complex aircraft.

FACO activities make up a relatively small portion of the total aircraft cost. Lockheed Martin estimates that the JSF FACO cost is about 2 percent of fleet unit recurring flyaway (URF) costs. Other airframe work totals 35 percent of costs, propulsion totals 19 percent, and other non-airframe items total 44 percent of URF costs.

The 2-percent figure is a lower FACO percentage than other recent programs have experienced. Historically, FACO has been a larger portion of the total manufacturing labor because most of the electronics and subsystems were integrated into the airframe during this stage. Also, old design and manufacturing approaches led to part and subassembly variability problems. Often these problems were discovered during final assembly and resulted in considerable

Table 1.2

Cycle Time Required for FACO Activities

Activity	Days to Complete
Structural mate	2.4
Subsystems mate and tail installation	4.8
Final assembly and systems test	12.0
Final finishes	10.8
Field operations	10.8
Total Workdays	40.8

rework. Thus, historically, the FACO percentage of the total labor has been higher than is projected for the JSF.

The FACO portion for the F-22 is 3.3 percent (not including engines and some support). Reports indicate that F/A-18E/F FACO percentage is higher still. The original F-22 production plan was to have all major assemblies arrive "fully stuffed" with all the components, subassemblies, avionics, and so forth, rather than have them installed during FACO. According to interviews with DoD personnel, there have been some difficulties during the initial production experience, with more work than expected taking place during FACO. Lockheed Martin managers have indicated that they are attempting to resolve associated issues. It is not uncommon to have to work through difficulties during initial production. In any case, advances in design technology and production and tooling approaches since the F-22 was originally designed may enable the JSF to meet its goals for FACO—but this is not guaranteed.

PURPOSE OF THE STUDY

The JSF Program Office and OSD asked RAND's National Defense Research Institute to conduct the study mandated by Congress, and to assess fully and objectively different FACO strategies. This report responds to that request. It details the different FACO strategies that were examined, the different sites that were selected, and how the costs of doing different portions of the work at different sites were assessed.

FACO Strategies

One of the first steps of our research was to identify different FACO strategies. The congressional language makes it clear that the acquisition strategies to be examined include an examination of allocating all or portions of FACO to different potential locations. RAND has identified a number of ways this allocation can occur.

The baseline FACO strategy, for cost comparison purposes, is to have all activities at a single site. As described above, these activities include substructures mating and assembly work, systems checkout, final finishing, and field operations. All of these tasks would take place at a single site for the entire life of the program, from SDD[10] through LRIP, to FRP. Unless directed otherwise by the U.S. government, Lockheed Martin plans to perform FACO at its Fort Worth location, Air Force Plant (AFP) 4. Company officials cite their capabilities there as the reason for the choice of that site, and the cost efficiencies of performing all FACO at a single location as the reason they do not plan to split the work.

But there are other ways to accomplish FACO. It could be done at multiple sites: two, three, or even more FACO sites could, conceivably, be operated. This approach would spread work across different locations, but each additional site would potentially add cost because of extra facilities requirements, along with the costs stemming from the multiple learning curves.

Multiple site approaches can vary by how the different JSF variants are distributed among the sites. One option is to build all of the variants at every site. Another option is to split the variants among sites, for example, assembling each variant at a separate site. Alternatively, one variant could be built at one site, and the other two variants could be built at another site.

Another option is to divide FACO activities among sites. For example, assembly could occur at one location and system checkout at another. Lockheed Martin has argued convincingly against separating these functions, citing, for example the cost and risk of shipping the aircraft at any period before flight-test. Because of the obvious and strong disadvantages of this strategy, it has not been analyzed further in this report.

A final set of alternatives in the division of FACO activities concerns the timing of adding new sites. One option is that all sites start up at the same time—at LRIP. Alternatively, second and third sites could be added at later dates in the program (for example, at the beginning of FRP).

To provide a range of possibilities across these alternatives, we present the results from an analysis of a sample of the possible universe.

---

[10]Terminology for the acquisition phases, as found in the DoD 5000 series of acquisition regulations, changed in 2001. SDD refers to what was previously known as Engineering and Manufacturing Development.

While these alternatives do not include all possibilities, we feel that the following represent the most reasonable:

1. 100 percent of FACO at Lockheed Martin–Fort Worth (baseline case).

2. 100 percent of FACO at Lockheed Martin–Palmdale (Calif.), at the beginning of LRIP.

3. 100 percent of FACO at Lockheed Martin–Marietta (Ga.), at the beginning of LRIP.

4. 100 percent of FACO at Northrop Grumman–Palmdale, at the beginning of LRIP.

5. 50 percent of FACO at Lockheed Martin–Fort Worth and 50 percent at Lockheed Martin–Palmdale, production starting in Fort Worth, then splitting at FRP.

6. 50 percent of FACO at Lockheed Martin–Fort Worth and 50 percent at Northrop Grumman–Palmdale, production starting in Fort Worth, then splitting at FRP.

7. 50 percent of FACO at Lockheed Martin–Fort Worth and 50 percent at Lockheed Martin–Marietta, production starting in Fort Worth, then splitting at FRP.

8. All CTOL at Lockheed Martin–Fort Worth and all CV and STOVL at Lockheed Martin–Marietta, variant production splitting at LRIP.

9. One-third of all production at each of the three Lockheed Martin sites, production starting in Fort Worth, then splitting at FRP.

We also provide results from analyses designed to test the sensitivity of these findings to different conditions, including different levels of transfer of learning across sites, different start dates for alternative sites, and the use of discounted net present value (NPV) instead of FY 2002 dollars.

Methodology

This research began approximately six months before the contract for SDD was awarded to Lockheed Martin on October 26, 2001.

During the months leading up to the SDD award, RAND collected general data on the specific issue areas called out by Congress, on other costs that would vary by location (e.g., energy), and on facilities, along with corporate data that were not source selection–sensitive. RAND began work on a cost model to estimate different costs of performing FACO at different sets of locations. The model can assess the costs of the different FACO strategies discussed above.

After the prime contractor selection, RAND engaged in a second round of data collection to populate the model with JSF program and other data. This period of the study was relatively compressed, with much data only becoming available in the remaining six weeks before this report was due. We identified a set of final potential FACO sites to be analyzed in the study, and collected specific costs pertaining to these locations. The cost model calculates FACO costs at different facilities, given the different FACO strategies. RAND also engaged the assistance of the Defense Contract Management Agency (DCMA) to conduct a site survey used to collect data specific to the different sites. This survey is provided in Appendix B.

Where specific cost information could not be collected, a description will be provided and the implications assessed. For example, one environmental issue is noise from acceptance flights. There is a risk that community activists could protest and create limitations on the times of day when aircraft can be flown. While this does not have a specific cost calculated for it, the potential implications are discussed.

HOW THIS REPORT IS ORGANIZED

This report is organized in 10 substantive chapters. Following this introduction, Chapter Two lays out the policy issues of alternate FACO strategies. It includes a brief history of programs with split production, and assesses rationales for splitting JSF FACO. Chapter Three describes facilities requirements for FACO and the approach we took to the selection of potential FACO sites. Chapters Four through Eight describe and assess the cost elements that vary for each site. Chapter Nine introduces the model used to evaluate the costs of performing FACO at different sites. Chapter Ten presents the results of the study; it also provides total cost estimates for a variety of FACO strategies and discusses the sensitivities of the results to key parameters. Finally, conclusions are presented in Chapter Eleven. In addition, Appendix A contains the language from the appropriations law directing this study; Appendix B includes the DCMA site survey; Appendix C contains a comparison of wages across potential FACO sites; and Appendix D describes some of the environmental legislation that affects the costs of establishing additional FACO sites.

Chapter Two

SPLITTING PRODUCTION

INTRODUCTION

While not prescribing a JSF FACO approach, the congressional language calling for this study required an examination of alternate FACO strategies. The language focused principally on various factors that would affect the cost at the different potential FACO sites. While cost is a predominant consideration, other issues must be explored as well to ensure an informed decision regarding the sharing of FACO activities among multiple sites.

This chapter initially focuses on issues relating to splitting production. In addition, it presents an overview of several policy considerations that will affect FACO strategy. Finally, this chapter provides an overview of historical examples of split production.

GENERAL POLICY ISSUES RELATED TO SPLITTING DEFENSE PRODUCTION

Several reasons are potentially valid for splitting any kind of defense production. The most common, from an acquisition viewpoint, is to generate competition to gain its attendant benefits. These benefits are generally thought to include better product performance, higher production efficiency and lower unit costs, and greater contractor responsiveness. While the JSF procurement will not incorporate competition, as will be discussed, it is useful to describe competition to clarify the issues involved in splitting FACO and how they will differ.

Classic market competition does not occur in the procurement of major defense systems: There are no cases where a large number of sellers provide similar goods and services to many buyers. In the defense industry, there is, usually, one major buyer and a limited number of sellers.

Given this environment, holding a true competition, where the contractor (seller) with the best value bid (lowest price and/or best performance) can win 100 percent of the business, has some distinct disadvantages. For example, the losing contractor must bear considerable costs at the conclusion of the competition—e.g., costs associated with laying off workers, having to rehire and retrain them later on. Furthermore, a contractor who loses the competition might be forced out of the business because of these costs. After that, the remaining contractor no longer faces the competition that works to keep costs down and value up. Hence, competition in the defense industry often features either directed buys, where the production is divided according to some predetermined formula, or a continued competition, e.g., where the work shared between two or more companies varies over time as a function of their performance.

Splitting production has associated costs. These include duplicate facilities and tooling, loss of learning economies, and increased overhead that occur when production is split between two or more sites.

The benefits and costs of splitting production in the procurement of major defense weapon systems have been repeatedly examined.[1] The question is whether the benefits of competition outweigh the additional costs. This has never been completely resolved. Indeed, the answer likely differs for different classes of weapon systems as well as in different individual procurements. It has even been shown that analyzing the effects of competition on costs for one weapon system using different methods can produce different results.[2]

Usually, the definition of "competition" is two or more separate organizations vying for sales to DoD, contrasted with a single con-

---

[1] For example, in Birkler et al., 2001; Birkler, Dews, and Large, 1990; and Birkler and Large, 1990.

[2] Birkler, Dews, and Large, 1990

tractor building one system. In reality, a range of alternatives can be found along a continuum (depicted in Figure 2.1) that can be labeled "level of competition," or, more accurately, "procurement production alternatives."

Each of these production alternatives has distinct features and involves the maintenance of a different set of skills by single or multiple companies.

Having multiple sources for any weapon system—"competition"— can take several forms. The fullest form of competition is to have completely different weapon systems that would support similar missions competing for government orders (the far right-hand side of Figure 2.1). These should have enough functional similarities that, to some extent, they can substitute for one another. The government theoretically has a choice, for example, in procuring more F-15Es versus more F-16s. In reality, many factors, from the different capabilities of the aircraft to the branch of the armed forces for which the aircraft was originally developed, shape the choice to a great extent. The companies involved in this competition have the most freedom in terms of design, program management, production approaches, and so forth.

Often the government already has an existing weapon system for which it wishes to develop competition. Given this, two alternatives exist when introducing competition in weapon system acquisition. One is to qualify a second source to develop a system that is func-

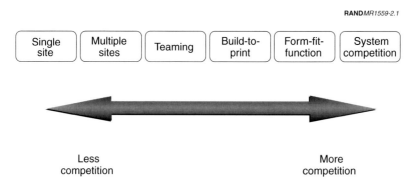

RAND*MR1559-2.1*

| Single site | Multiple sites | Teaming | Build-to-print | Form-fit-function | System competition |

Less competition   More competition

Figure 2.1—Continuum of Procurement Production Alternatives

tionally the same but with a different design, known as a "form-fit-function" approach. The goal is for the two systems to be essentially substitutable for each other because their capabilities and performance would be identical from the user's perspective. The form-fit-function approach can be expensive because it essentially duplicates the effort involved in the development process while limiting the ability to provide new capabilities or design approaches. The second source is given fixed specifics to design to, reducing alternatives, and must shape its own internal capabilities and expertise to develop something functionally the same as that developed by a firm with different capabilities and approaches to design. At the same time, the second source does maintain independent design and program integration expertise. Military engines are an example of this kind of market, where the government can pick between Pratt & Whitney and General Electric Aircraft Engines versions of the same engine.

The other approach is the "build-to-print" method, where the second contractor builds the same system as the prime contractor. This is also known as the "leader-follower" approach. The original prime contractor must share the blueprints and various processes with the second source, which may raise some intellectual property issues. The goal is to have an identical weapon system. A downside is that the second source likely will not participate in the design process. The second source does decide how to organize production and the supply chain, not necessarily duplicating all of the prime contractor's choices. This approach has been followed in developing second sources for missiles. For example, the original producer of the Tomahawk missile was General Dynamics/Convair, with McDonnell Douglas integrating the guidance system. At the government's request, the contractors shared technical information so that each could produce the identical missile.[3]

Each of these three approaches (system competition, form-fit-function, and build-to-print) involves the sort of competition not under consideration here, as will be discussed below. The alternatives considered in this study are: teaming with multiple sites, one contractor with multiple sites, and one contractor with a single site.

---

[3]Birkler and Large, 1990.

One production alternative is to have a second company do some of the work but have the two companies participate in a "teaming" arrangement.[4] Here, designs and processes are shared as well as the organization of production and the supply chain. A single contract may be used to purchase procured goods and services for both manufacturers. A second team of company managers is involved in the work and in program management but does not develop an original approach. Two sets of industrial engineers can analyze the work. Some duplication of effort is involved, but this is limited.

In a second alternative, a single company may choose to split production between two sites that it controls.[5] This may be done for capacity or for some other reason. Here, the duplication is even more limited, specifically, of the two teams of workers skilled at doing the same kind of work, as well as some duplication of manufacturing engineers.

Finally, the most restricted production alternative, on the far left-hand side of Figure 2.1, is a single company building all units at a single site. Here, there is one design team, one program management team, one plant management group, one set of manufacturing and industrial engineers, and one group of workers performing the labor.

The production alternatives are summarized in Table 2.1.

JSF

With a single weapon system under consideration, true competition between the JSF and some other system is not at issue here. From the outset, the acquisition strategy for the JSF has differed from either the form-fit-function or build-to-print approaches. The goal of those two approaches is to garner the benefits of competition by letting the firms compete for some of or the entire buy. From the beginning of the CDP, DoD tried to induce the best efforts from the

---

[4]This is the third alternative from the left on the continuum of procurement production alternatives.

[5]This is the second alternative from the left.

Table 2.1

Skills Maintained by Range of Production Alternatives

Alternative	Design Engineering	Program Management/ Integration	Production/ Mechanical Engineering	Touch Labor
System competition	Multiple independent teams	Multiple independent teams	Multiple independent teams	Multiple, with independent skills
Form-fit-function	Independent design, but to constrained specifications	Multiple independent teams	Multiple independent teams	Multiple, with independent skills
Build-to-print	Single	Multiple independent teams	Multiple independent teams	Multiple, with independent skills, may have same management approach
Teaming	Single	Multiple teams, second team has limited impact	Multiple, with interaction and sharing	Multiple, with independent skills, same management approach
Multiple sites	Single	Single	Some duplication	Multiple, with independent skills
Single site	Single	Single	Single	Single

contractors by awarding the JSF as a winner-take-all program. The winner, if it so desired, would be able to bring the losing contractor onto the program, possibly to gain capabilities or even to win support for the program from Congress. Whether this cooperation would take place at all, as well as what activities the losing contractor would perform, would be negotiated by the contractors themselves and not directed by DoD. The goal of the program has been to have one contractor completely responsible for producing the weapon system.

For reasons that appear in the next chapter, this report examines only locations that either Lockheed Martin or Lockheed Martin with its JSF partner, Northrop Grumman Air Combat Systems, control.

This approach to FACO of the JSF corresponds to the "single site," "multiple sites," and "teaming" alternatives described above. (A complete description of the site-selection process appears in Chapter Three.) The participating companies would not be in competition with each other, so they would not have the incentives that competition generates in an open market. At the same time, the partners should be willing to share lessons learned, so some of the learning could transfer between sites. Sites under consideration include Lockheed Martin facilities in Fort Worth, Marietta, and at Site 10 in Palmdale, along with Northrop Grumman's Sites 3 and 4 in Palmdale.

ARGUMENTS FOR AND AGAINST SPLITTING PRODUCTION

A directed split of final assembly and checkout between two different locations controlled by the same firm or by a firm and a partner organization would be a new arrangement for modern aircraft procurement. An assessment of the costs and benefits reveals that the costs can usually be better estimated than the benefits, which often take an intangible form. In this report, we use the RAND cost model to address the cost issue. The analysis is described in Chapter Ten. In this chapter, we assess the intangible benefits typically cited in support of having competition or multiple sites in weapon systems procurement programs: contractor performance, industrial base, capacity, risk, buffer, and the sharing of economic benefits.

Contractor Performance

The JSF competition was structured so that a single prime contractor (which turned out to be Lockheed Martin), would win the JSF. Even if the decision were made to develop multiple FACO sites, there would be no competition between the sites in the traditional sense. Hence, it is RAND's estimation that splitting FACO would not create the benefits of competition in its classic sense, which include better product performance, higher production efficiency along with lower unit costs, and greater contractor responsiveness, as distinct competitors fight to increase their market share. Even without traditional competition, it is conceivable that a type of cost competition could be set up in house, with each site being encouraged to be more efficient than the others. Employees could be offered incentives to win the "competition." Merely tracking and publicly reporting which plant did better could result in a Hawthorne effect[6] that could improve local performance.

However, incentives in defense production for cost savings by the contractor are limited, potentially limiting the willingness of firms to create this kind of in-house competition. Even firm-fixed-price contracts are often based on the previous year's cost. Cost-based contracts provide a disincentive to cut costs. These contract types may have slowed the adoption of industrial best practices by the defense industry.[7] Furthermore, and more dangerously, if the sites competed with each other, it is less likely that they would share learning. Knowing that their performances are being directly compared could make the sites less willing to share lessons learned and process improvements with each other. This could result in costs from loss of learning that might even outweigh potential benefits from this staged competition. If different sites gradually developed different approaches that they did not share with each other, the result could be a kind of "configuration drift," as the aircraft built at the different sites became less common. (This would be a risk even though there presumably would be conscious effort on the part of DoD to manage this.) The result of less commonality could be greater life-cycle costs.

One reason cited in historical cases for adding a second source in weapon procurements is insufficient or even bad performance by the initial prime contractor. The F-100 engine is an oft-cited example of this. According to some sources, Pratt & Whitney was unresponsive to its most important customer—DoD, which then developed General Electric Aircraft Engines as a second source.[8] Better contractor performance is one of the benefits of competition. However, dividing JSF FACO activities among the sites considered in this research would not create or reflect a competitive situation. Although there may be variation in performance, having a single corporate management team interacting with the customer would mean individual

---

[6]Researchers investigating ways to improve worker performance noted that management attention led workers to increase their effort. This research was conducted at the Western Electric plant in Hawthorne, Ill., in the 1930s (Roethlisberger and Dickson, 1939; Mayo, 1945).

[7]See, for example, Cook and Graser, 2001.

[8]For example, Drewes, 1987.

sites would not necessarily make attempts to be more responsive—or less costly—than the other sites.[9]

Industrial Base

According to current procurement plans, when the F-22 and the F/A-18E/F finish production, the JSF will be the only manned tactical aircraft still being built for the U.S. military (see Figure 2.2). While follow-on orders and orders for foreign military sales may keep the other production lines active after production is scheduled to close, these future orders are unknown. Some in Congress and elsewhere have expressed the concern that having a single tactical aircraft production line with no competition will result in an unacceptable diminution of the tactical aircraft industrial base.

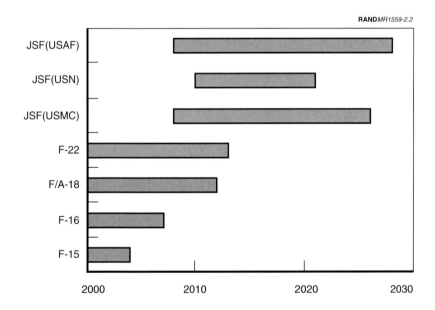

Figure 2.2—Fighter Aircraft Production Schedules

---

[9]Although Lockheed Martin would certainly have the opportunity to put in place internal corporate incentives to this effect.

The industrial base issue of manned tactical aircraft has been the subject of considerable concern and has been studied repeatedly. In 2002, Congress mandated a new study to look at the strength of the U.S. military aircraft industrial base for all types of aircraft.

In the meantime, this report will address what capabilities FACO sustains and whether having two JSF FACO sites is necessary or preferable in light of those capabilities. One way to approach this issue is to break down the industrial base for tactical aircraft into its component capabilities and assess how well alternate production plans sustain these capabilities. These varied capabilities include overall program management; design and development of aircraft; managing the integration of aircraft, including managing a supplier industrial base; manufacturing and support engineering; and performing the actual labor involved with final assembly and checkout, as appears, for example, in Table 2.1. Certainly, the loss of capability in aircraft design or overall aircraft and program management integration could be a concern if there were only one producer of tactical aircraft (although there is room for disagreement even here). Usually, these are viewed as the most critical capabilities to maintain.

Splitting JSF FACO across two sites owned by the same firm or by teammates who worked on the aircraft development and program integration together, would not maintain the most critical capabilities—design and program integration. The work that would be duplicated includes predominantly touch labor and some support labor, including quality control and engineering. Furthermore, the work involved in JSF FACO is not unique. These manufacturing skills will be supported by work on other aircraft programs, including both manned and unmanned vehicles, and by maintenance activities throughout the life of the aircraft. One company's assessment was that, while routine depot maintenance checkout is a factor of 10 less complicated than that involved in initial production, if a problem with the aircraft cropped up during depot maintenance, many more of the initial production tasks would be duplicated and the work would approach initial checkout activities.

Avoidance of Risk

Having two or more FACO sites could reduce the risk of losing production capability in the event of a natural disaster or a terrorist attack. Certainly natural disasters cannot be planned for, although in areas of known natural risk, such as Southern California, building codes can mitigate the risk of some disasters, e.g., earthquakes.

Industrial facilities generally do not make good targets for terrorists. One expert on terrorism[10] assessed the risk of an attack on an industrial location that is not also a major U.S. symbol (such as the World Trade Center was) as low, because targeting industrial resources is highly unusual for insurgent groups. Leftist groups may have been more likely to do so if the site was seen as symbolic of the capitalist system, but this risk has substantially diminished in recent years. Furthermore, splitting FACO does not control the risk that the attack may occur on the critical subcomponent level. Also, security can help mitigate man-made disasters.

Capacity

As discussed below, North American and Boeing produced post–World War II military aircraft (F-86, F-100, B-52) at multiple locations partly for capacity reasons.[11] A large number of these aircraft were needed quickly for the Cold War. While the JSF program does call for the production of a large number of aircraft, it is spread out over 20 years, reducing the pressure on the capacity of any one plant.

Furthermore, the general approach to aircraft manufacturing has changed dramatically since the 1950s. Then, the producer actually fabricated many of the parts for the aircraft, put together the smaller subassemblies, and then assembled them into an integrated whole. Now, the majority of the final product is generally procured from subcontractors. Prime contractors tend to focus on integrating assemblies and subassemblies, making it less likely that having a

---

[10]Daniel Byman, RAND, interviewed February 15, 2002.

[11]Another reason for the 2nd protection sites away from the coast may have been to protect against a sea-based attack. With the development of more-powerful intercontinental ballistic missiles, however, even production sites in the middle of the country are vulnerable.

single location would create an unacceptable limit on production capacity. The sites considered in this analysis (to be discussed) operate one-and-a-half to two shifts, with a support shift at night. If more capacity were needed, they could each add a full third shift.

Finally, studies have shown that the aircraft industry currently has excess production capacity.[12] The existing capacity at the major aircraft manufacturing sites means splitting FACO is unlikely to be needed to meet capacity requirements. Chapter Three shows the facilities and investment increases needed at the candidate FACO sites to support full-rate JSF production—they are small.

Strategic Buffer

The issue of maintaining an adequate buffer in production is related to the capacity issue. Here, the goal is to maintain facilities and expert workforces at both sites so that if a surge in production capacity were suddenly needed, two trained workforces would be available to handle it. This could be required if a serious global competitor building up its own tactical aircraft capacity arose, if smaller contingencies requiring tactical aircraft response increased, or if mission requirements changed.

Several counterarguments weigh against the strategic buffer approach. First, it is highly unlikely that a strategic competitor would arise so quickly that production at the first FACO facility could not speed up in time or that a second line could not be added elsewhere in response to the threat. U.S. intelligence would likely be able to ascertain if a country were building up its tactical aircraft capacity in time for the United States to counter. An increase in small contingencies is more likely, but the level of the increase in FACO that would be required in this case is not clear. As far as changing mission requirements, generally this is a longer-term process that can be met with the usual procurement procedures.

Furthermore, the long lead time on many procured items going into the subassemblies means that a speedy increase of FACO would be

_____
[12]Gholz and Sapolsky, 1999/2000.

very difficult unless an increase in capacity were developed for the entire JSF value stream, not just for FACO.

Share Economic Benefit

An argument can be made that defense production is not the same as commercial production. In commercial production, maximizing profit is usually the overriding goal. Defense production has a public policy component. Even if inefficiencies result from splitting FACO, there may be policy reasons to do so, such as sharing the economic benefit from a major weapon system program. Splitting FACO could mean that two or more communities get these benefits, rather than just one.

The currently planned JSF program is large. Although FACO activities make up a small portion of the total, around 2 percent, they still amount to several billion dollars for the planned 3,002 production run, and more if additional exports occur. Having multiple FACO sites would share the economic benefits among more communities. If FACO is spread across locations, two or multiple communities will maintain major final assembly lines, complete with multiple skilled labor forces. If the work is split, the initial site will lose some jobs as the second site gains them.

Splitting production does not come without costs, which we will describe later. Each additional site will require the facilities, equipment, and tooling needed to perform FACO operations. Furthermore, spreading production among multiple sites means that the efficiency benefits from learning will likely be reduced. The result will be more labor hours and more workers required to perform FACO.

The additional facilities, equipment, tooling, labor hours, and workers directly translate into increased costs for the total weapon system without a concurrent improvement in warfighting capability. These costs must be covered somehow, and are, by the taxes that citizens in all communities pay. In Chapter Ten, we estimate the differential costs of splitting FACO. As will be seen, they are rather small when compared with the cost of the total program, but are still significant in their own right. It is a policy decision on the part of the U.S. government to determine whether the economic benefits from sharing FACO across multiple sites outweigh these costs.

Note also that production for the JSF is already spread across the United States. Many states participate in the production of sub-assemblies and components (see Figure 2.3). Subcontractors to these suppliers are further distributed across the United States.

Finally, because a decision to split FACO to spread the economic benefit might take into account economically depressed areas, we provide the December 2001 unemployment rates[13] at the following three potential FACO sites considered in this report:

- Palmdale: 5.7 percent (average monthly rate for 2001—5.5 percent).

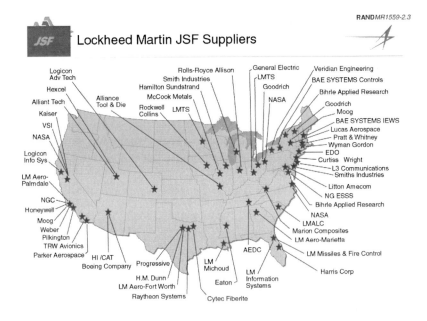

SOURCE: Lockheed Martin Aeronautics Company.

Figure 2.3—States with Significant Involvement in JSF Production

---

[13]http://www.bls.gov.

- Fort Worth: 4.7 percent (average monthly rate for 2001—3.68 percent).

- Marietta: 4.2 percent (average monthly rate for 2001—3.4 percent).

The average national unemployment rate was 4.8 percent in 2001. While Palmdale has a higher unemployment rate than the other two locations, its unemployment rate does not indicate a depressed economy.

To summarize, splitting FACO would benefit more than one locality, but this benefit comes at a cost to all taxpayers and may affect the ability of DoD to invest its resources into the military capabilities that it needs. Significant JSF work is already spread throughout the country, benefiting a number of local communities. None of the areas under consideration for FACO has serious economic problems. Hence, the need to share economic benefits further does not appear to be a compelling reason to split FACO activities among multiple sites.

THE U.S. EXPERIENCE

The United States has limited postwar experience with multisite production of aircraft. In fact, no aircraft in production is undergoing final assembly at multiple sites. This holds true for commercial[14] as well as for military aircraft. There are some instances of split production from other defense systems, such as missiles and ships. The following summary does not attempt to be an exhaustive review of all of the cases.

Three Post–World War II Aircraft: F-86, F-100, and B-52

Three examples of post–World War II aircraft built in two locations within the United States are the North American F-86 Sabre and F-100 Super Sabre and the Boeing B-52. Production for both the F-86 and F-100 began in Southern California, and second production lines

---

[14]If multiple sites offered economic benefits, presumably, profit-seeking commercial manufacturers would split their production.

were later opened for both aircraft in Columbus, Ohio. The B-52 was produced first in Seattle, Wash.; later, production took place in both Seattle and Wichita, Kan., concurrently.[15] In all of these cases, the prime contractor controlled both sites.

Rich et al. (1981, pp. 61–66) present evidence on how different categories of costs of the F-100 and the B-52 programs were affected by having multiple production sites for the aircraft. For engineering, the B-52's second site required about a 10-percent increase in the hours required to produce the 172 aircraft manufactured in Wichita. For the F-100, however, engineering hours to produce the 359 aircraft at the second site actually declined by about 48 percent. Rich et al. postulate that a smaller fixed engineering staff at the second site explains the reduction in cost, but the savings could have been driven by a design that was easier to produce or by some other factor.

For both the F-100 and the B-52, tooling requirements for the second facilities were significant and added substantial costs. Nonrecurring tooling hours for the F-100 at Columbus were 96 percent of those required for the work in Los Angeles, even though the maximum production rate was 40-percent less. If costs are scaled for production runs of the same size, nonrecurring tooling hours would have increased by 344 percent at the second site for B-52s and by 388 percent for F-100s. The authors report that for manufacturing, producing at two facilities rather than extending the original production at the original site led to a significant increase in manufacturing labor hours. They also note that increases in material costs associated with multiple sites can be kept to a minimum if purchasing is centralized or coordinated.

Rich and his coauthors note that indirect costs, including overhead and general and administrative costs, make up a large portion of the cost of any aircraft. Each facility generally has its own overhead rates, although some companies[16] have moved to consolidate as many of these costs as possible across locations to develop a single overhead rate or at least rates more similar across sites. The authors

---

[15]Rich et al., 1981, p. 61.

[16]Including Lockheed Martin, which has consolidated its Fort Worth, Marietta, and Palmdale facilities into one unit—the Lockheed Martin Aeronautics Company—headquartered in Fort Worth.

argue that moving production to a site with a lower overhead rate may result in overall savings if the reduction in cost exceeds the increase in overhead costs that will result at the first facility.

While the B-52 and F-100 offer interesting examples of multisite productions, lessons may be limited for aircraft developed and produced some 50 years later. Vastly different design philosophies, manufacturing technologies, and communication technologies between sites make direct comparison in the search for lessons learned problematic. For example, aircraft manufacturers in the 1950s tended to do much more of the work on site compared with current practice. Today, aircraft assemblers are much more likely to contract out parts and subcomponents and act more as integrators than as fabricators.

Coproduction of an Aircraft

Split production of the same aircraft has often been done because overseas production lines have been established either to encourage overseas sales or as a condition of such sales. Rich et al. (1981, pp. 131–133) present an exhaustive list of aerospace systems (including fixed-wing aircraft, helicopters, and missiles, along with tanks, howitzers, armored vehicles, and projectiles) that had been coproduced in multiple countries from World War II until that report's publication. The many examples of aircraft produced abroad as well as in the United States include the F-86, F-104, F-4, F-15, F-16, and AV-8A/B. (This last aircraft, also known as the Harrier, was first produced in the United Kingdom and later in St. Louis by McDonnell.)

The F-16 aircraft is probably the most comparable to the single-engine JSF (its ultimate replacement). F-16 aircraft final assembly took place in the Netherlands by Fokker; in Belgium by SABCA; in Turkey by TUSAS Aerospace Industries; in South Korea by Samsung Aircraft; as well as in Fort Worth. Despite the lower wages paid at several of these locations, the international production of the F-16, in the opinion of Lockheed Martin personnel interviewed by RAND, was never done for efficiency reasons. Rather, the governments in the countries where this work was performed were concerned about their own industrial base and with developing certain capabilities, in spite of the cost premium. According to previous RAND research,

"Belgian officials admit that direct purchase would be about 10 percent cheaper" than having a local production line.[17] However, if additional jobs were created in Belgium by Belgian F-16 production, the resulting taxes may have meant that the Belgian government saved money by producing it domestically.

THE EUROPEAN EXPERIENCE

Another example of multinational production is offered by the new all-European fighter, the EF-2000 Typhoon (the Eurofighter) aircraft, which will be produced by a consortium of manufacturers in four countries: the United Kingdom, Germany, Italy, and Spain. Each nation will manufacture different components, and each will have its own final assembly sites. Production workshares will be specifically related to the number of aircraft ordered by each partner nation (232 for the United Kingdom, 180 for Germany, 121 for Italy, and 87 for Spain). BAE Systems will assemble the UK version in Warton; Alenia Aerospazio, a Finmeccanica company, will assemble the Italian aircraft in Turin; Construcciones Aeronáuticas S.A. will assemble the Spanish aircraft in Madrid; and DaimlerChrysler Aerospace AG will assemble the German aircraft in Munich. These last two companies, also known as CASA and DASA, are part of the multinational defense consortium EADS (European Aeronautic Defence and Space Company).

Unquestionably the costs of producing the Eurofighter at multiple locations will be greater than if there was a single final assembly line. According to Latham (1989, p. 101),

> All four participating countries plan to establish their own final assembly lines, and this will necessarily tend to reduce the benefits derived from specialisation. However, as final assembly typically accounts for only about 10 percent of European production costs, the collaboration premia associated with duplication can be as little as 1 to 2 percent of final production expenditures.

---

[17]Rich et al., 1984.

Later evidence[18] suggests that the costs of EF-2000 FACO will be even lower, on the order of 4 percent, so any cost of duplication of final assembly lines would be scaled by that smaller amount. Having separate final assembly lines may raise costs for each nation, but the FACO activities are seen as critical to developing an adequate maintenance capability for the aircraft, as some of the activities and relevant experience overlap. And because each nation plans to maintain its own aircraft, multiple FACO lines may be the most reasonable approach to developing this capability.

Collaborating on a cross-national program is significantly less expensive than having individual national programs, as Latham (1989, p. 101) argues:

> Considering both the benefits derived from scale and learning economies and the penalties associated with duplication, it would seem that a base order of 800 units for the EFA program could be expected to reduce unit costs by as much as 30 percent of the cost of a national program (although 15 to 20 percent is perhaps a more reasonable estimate).

COPRODUCTION OF NAVY SYSTEMS BY MULTIPLE CONTRACTORS

While no current examples of U.S. aircraft are undergoing final assembly at multiple locations, other defense programs have multiple final assembly locations, and these might provide useful lessons for a multisite FACO strategy for the JSF. The production of ships and submarines for the U.S. Navy probably offers the most similarities because they are very complex weapon systems. Four are particularly notable. The DDG-51 *Arleigh Burke* destroyer is being produced at both General Dynamics Bath Iron Works in Maine and Northrop Grumman Ship Systems Ingalls Operations in Mississippi. The original program structure of LPD-17 Landing Platform Dock had it being manufactured at General Dynamics Bath Iron Works in Maine and Northrop Grumman Ship Systems Avondale Operations in New Orleans. *Virginia*-class submarine (SSN-774) production is

---

[18]Interview conducted in 1999 by Katia Vlachos with a senior manager at Eurofighter GmbH.

split between Electric Boat in Connecticut and Northrop Grumman Newport News in Virginia. Each company is responsible for unique modules; final assembly alternates between the two shipyards. The production of the *Los Angeles*–class submarines (SSN-688) was also split between these two shipyards.[19]

We interviewed individuals in the Navy and Office of the Secretary of Defense who were involved with these four programs. There was some disagreement about the reasons these programs had split production. Industrial base issues, the benefits of competition (including lower costs or reduced cost growth), and pure politics were all cited as reasons for the splits, and all probably hold true to some extent. Some capacity issues may exist in shipbuilding as well because the shipyards have a limited number of docks. Whether these limitations truly required the splitting of production for these ships is not clear.

Our interviews revealed a number of production and management issues. While shipyards produce the ships from the same blueprint (and thus should be producing indistinguishable systems), some individuals claim they can easily spot the difference between ships and submarines built by different producers, although these differences are thought to be cosmetic. Another difference is the production techniques employed by different shipyards. One such example is the bending or welding of pipes. One shipyard tends to bend pipes, while the other prefers to weld sections of straight pipe with elbow joints. When changes in design occur, each shipyard has to incorporate the change into its approach, thus adding time and cost.

Sharing information among sites is not always easy. One lesson learned painfully over time was the importance of having compatible design and analysis tools (i.e., for CAD/CAM). Programs with two production locations ran into difficulties when they used different systems. There was consensus that all ship manufacturers were considering CATIA[20] as their standard CAD/CAM program, so this problem should decrease in the future. But even when these use identical systems, the translation issues mentioned above can create

---

[19]Other Navy examples include the *Seawolf* submarine (SSN-21), the FFG-7, and some sealift ships.

[20]A design and analysis tool originally developed by Dassault Systemes.

problems if the two companies have different approaches to manufacturing.

An amicable business relationship is important for sharing lessons learned across sites. During our interviews, we learned of cases in which the two corporate managements could not effectively work together, and thus the Navy had to step in to resolve various issues. People from the different companies who worked together directly at the shipyard usually had good working relationships. However, because these sites are not partners, but rather, direct competitors, some concern arose that they would not share all manufacturing experience, which would reduce overall cost or improve performance for all ships being delivered to the Navy. The competitors must share formal ECPs/ECOs,[21] however, they need not share informal lessons learned.

Whatever the original reasons for splitting the production of the ships, one split has recently come under some question. The Navy, Northrop Grumman, and General Dynamics agreed that the two exchange work so that each focuses more on one program.[22] Under this agreement, Northrop Grumman will give up four of its DDG-51 destroyers, which instead will be built by General Dynamics at Bath Iron Works in Maine. In return, Bath Iron Works will give up four LPD-17 amphibious ships. Some DDG-51s will still likely be built by Northrop Grumman. *Inside the Navy* reports, "the Navy maintains it will reap significant savings in the LPD-17 program by giving one company production of all 12 ships in the class, thus eliminating separate four-ship and eight-ship LPD-17 learning curves at two competing shipyards."[23] In short, the Navy presumably assumes that savings from a single learning curve will be greater than whatever savings competition would have generated.

The history of split production reflects different rationales. Production may be split because one plant does not have adequate capacity to produce the number of systems needed or because of industrial

---

[21]Engineering Change Proposals/Engineering Change Orders.

[22]"Shipbuilding Giants . . .," 2002; "Navy, GD and Northrop Cement . . .," 2002. Also see Darce, 2002.

[23]"Navy, GD and Northrop Cement . . .," 2002.

base considerations. The cost of establishing a second facility and the learning curve costs incurred at the new facility typically increase overall production costs, although one contact argued that competition has helped control contractor cost growth, even if no reductions in cost are obvious.

CONCLUSION

Historical experience with multiple production sites for weapon system production indicates that the approach increases costs. While several arguments other than cost can be made for requiring multiple sites for JSF FACO operations, they are not individually or collectively compelling.

The trend in government management of the defense business has been to reduce the amount of oversight and government control. The driving concept of performance-based contracting practices is that telling defense contractors the performance required of the desired weapon system rather than specifically telling them how to build it will encourage them to use their ingenuity to meet government needs most effectively. Requiring Lockheed Martin to split JSF FACO functions among different sites would therefore go against the spirit of acquisition reform.

However, the government might decide that the benefits of splitting FACO outweigh its costs. That is a policy question for the appropriate decisionmakers to address. This research has revealed no compelling case for benefits in support of splitting FACO.

Chapter Three

SITE SELECTION ISSUES: PLANT AND MAJOR
FACILITY REQUIREMENTS FOR FACO

The congressional language requiring this study calls for the identification of each government and industry facility that is a potential site for JSF FACO. Many factors require consideration when selecting an appropriate location for FACO activities. Industrial engineers include manufacturing requirements, specifics of the site, and external local and state issues when making their selection.[1] In this chapter, we describe the general considerations for selection of the FACO site, followed by a discussion of the sites that RAND considers to have reasonable potential. This chapter also provides details regarding the major plant and facility for any FACO location, whether a single or multiple site FACO strategy is used.

We present a discussion of a theoretical approach to site selection that addresses the question of how the universe of potential sites can be whittled down to those that are reasonable. The most practical approach would be selecting a site or sites with a current military aircraft production line that has sufficient capacity to accommodate JSF FACO operations. Within that subset, the most reasonable candidate sites would be those controlled by either Lockheed Martin Aeronautics Company or its partner, Northrop Grumman Air Combat Systems. This approach selects the candidate sites from among the most practical and meets direction provided by the JSF Program Office.

---

[1]Tompkins, 2001.

37

SPECIFIC SITE PHYSICAL REQUIREMENTS

According to Lockheed Martin, the specific plant and major facilities required to conduct JSF FACO at any given site are as follows:

- A runway at least 8,000 × 150 ft.

- A published, FAA-approved instrument approach and controlled airfield environment.

- Arresting gear.

- Taxiways and sufficient ramp space.

- An environmentally conditioned assembly building of approximately 130,000 sq ft (which includes assembly storage and office space).

- An environmentally controlled paint facility (this may be a section of the main assembly building).

- A low-observable testing and verification building (or section of the main assembly building).

- An aircraft flight operations run building (or section of the main assembly building).

- A "hover pad" and a hover pit for ground operation of the STOVL variants.

- Road access from the interstate highway system.

- Sufficient reliable and economical electrical power for all FACO operations.

CATEGORIES OF FACO OPTIONS

Given these requirements, DoD has at least five options for selecting an alternate location for JSF FACO activities. In roughly descending order, according to the number of potential sites (as well as cost to the government), these are as follows:

1. Constructing an airfield with new plant and facilities on a site not previously used for such a purpose (a "greenfield" site).

2. Selecting a site with an appropriate airfield, but without existing plant and facilities capable of supporting JSF FACO operations.

3. Selecting a site with an appropriate airfield, and with existing plant and facilities capable of supporting JSF FACO operations.

4. Selecting a site with an appropriate airfield, and with a current DoD operational or depot activity with excess plant and facilities capable of supporting JSF FACO operations.

5. Selecting a site with an appropriate airfield, and with a current military aircraft production or modification line with excess plant and facilities capable of supporting JSF FACO operations.

What follows is a discussion of each of these approaches, along with their benefits and cost. There is some repetition of the advantages and disadvantages among the alternatives.

Option 1: A "Greenfield" Site

Although there are recent examples (such as Denver International Airport) of airport construction at a "greenfield"[2] site, this has proved to be a very expensive process. RAND considers this option highly risky from a JSF schedule viewpoint and does not consider the greenfield option to be cost-effective for JSF FACO, especially given the supply of underutilized airfields currently supporting aircraft production, DoD operations, or logistics activities. U.S. Secretary of Transportation Norman Y. Mineta has noted that adding a runway to an existing airfield can take as long as 10 years.[3] In fact, it took 16 years for the Memphis–Shelby County Airport Authority to receive approval and construct two runways. In addition, the estimated cost of an additional runway at existing airports ranges from $76 million for a runway at Boston Logan to $1.156 billion at Lambert–St. Louis International Airport (which includes acquisition of additional property).[4] The average cost of 14 "critical" runways planned or under construction at existing airports in the United States is just under

---

[2]That is, a site where there are no facilities whatsoever—literally a green field.

[3]Mineta, 2001.

[4]Cho, 2001.

$400 million.[5] This approach would almost certainly be the most costly and time-consuming alternative to satisfying JSF requirements, especially in the early stages of production, and adds considerable schedule and cost risk to the program. However, it does have some advantages:

- Hundreds or even thousands of candidate sites could be considered.

- The latest designs and technology could be incorporated into the location.

- A site where the economic benefits from the work could help a faltering economy—for example, one with chronically high unemployment—could be selected.

- The site could maximize state and local tax incentives.

- The site could be placed where noise and environmental considerations would be negligible.

However, in addition to the initial cost and schedule risk, a greenfield site has several disadvantages:

- It could require significant regulatory action including environmental and Federal Aviation Administration (FAA) approvals as well as long lead time for airfield construction.

- It requires creating an entire airfield environment encompassing instrument approaches for a required capacity of less than 10 JSF flights per day.

- It adds to existing overcapacity in the aircraft industry.

- The entire cost of operating the airfield would be borne by the JSF FACO, unless other commercial or DoD uses could be found.

- There would be no sharing of overhead, security, and other support costs with other DoD programs.

---

[5]Airports with planned runways or runways already under construction are in Detroit, Miami, Orlando, Houston, Denver, Minneapolis, Charlotte, Atlanta, Boston, Cincinnati, Seattle, St. Louis, Washington (Dulles), and Dallas (Cho, 2001).

In terms of new facilities costs to create an alternative site to the Fort Worth facility, we estimate that the cost of this option would far outweigh the amount of work that JSF FACO represents. A few billion dollars of FACO activity spread over 20 years does not justify the likely costs and especially the schedule risks involved in this approach.

Option 2: A Site with an Existing Airfield Only

This option would involve the use of an existing U.S. civil airfield capable of handling jet aircraft that has a runway and taxiways sufficient to meet JSF requirements, but also one that currently does not have appropriate ramp space, buildings, and other facilities for FACO operations. Research[6] has revealed that there are approximately 375 airfields within the continental United States (CONUS) with runways of at least 8,000 ft in length and widths of 150 ft or more and FAA or military airspace controls. This option shares some of the advantages of a greenfield site in addition to some others:

- Hundreds of sites in the United States would be candidates.

- The latest designs and technology could be incorporated into the buildings and other facilities constructed.

- A site where the economic benefits from the work could help a faltering economy—for example, one with chronically high unemployment—could be selected.

- State and local tax incentives might be available.

- A site with relatively few regulatory restrictions, such as noise and environmental, could be chosen, although it might still require some regulatory approvals.

- The costs of operating the airfield could be shared with activities or organizations already there.

However, this option also has several disadvantages:

_____

[6]NIMA, 2001; U.S. Department of Transportation, 2001.

- It could require significant construction effort for additional ramp space, buildings, and other facilities.

- If it were a nonactive airfield, the costs to reopen and refurbish the facilities would be significant.

- It adds to existing overcapacity in the aircraft manufacturing industry.

- It provides for no sharing of overhead, security, and other support costs with other DoD programs.

Option 3: An Airfield with Existing Buildings Capable of Supporting JSF FACO

This option would involve the use of an existing U.S. civil airfield (or closed DoD or commercial airfield) capable of handling jet aircraft that has a runway, taxiways, and ramp and building space sufficient to meet most JSF requirements. Some minor construction or refurbishment might be required to the airfield or buildings to make them suitable for JSF FACO operations. Assessing the facilities available at each of the 375 airfields was both impractical and beyond the scope of this study. However, given knowledge of the existing facilities and using a generic list of facilities and equipment costs, an estimate of the required investment at each site could be developed, after the availability and condition of facilities at a site were determined.

Although this option somewhat narrows the number of candidate airfields, compared with the second option, it has some of the same advantages:

- While the exact number of sites that fall into this category cannot be determined without site surveys, we believe that dozens of sites in CONUS would be candidates.

- A site where the economic benefits from the work could help a faltering economy—for example, one with chronically high unemployment—could be selected.

- State and local tax incentives might be available.

- A site with relatively few regulatory restrictions, such as noise and environmental, could be chosen, although it could still require some regulatory approvals.

- The costs of operating the airfield could be shared with activities or organizations already there, if it were an active airfield.

However, many of the same disadvantages remain:

- It could require some new regulatory approvals, especially environmental ones, particularly if the airfield were not active.

- If it were an inactive airfield, the costs to reopen and refurbish the facilities would be significant.

- Developing the capacity to conduct JSF FACO at a new site would add to existing overcapacity in aircraft industry.

- It provides for no sharing of overhead, security, and other support costs with other DoD programs.

Option 4: A Site with a Current DoD Operation or Depot Activity with Excess Building Capacity

This option would involve placing JSF FACO at one of the 188[7] airfields in CONUS that has an active-duty, reserve, National Guard, or DoD depot organization present. The site(s) selected would have existing, underutilized building space so only minor construction would be necessary to accommodate FACO operations. This option offers the opportunity for the JSF FACO operation to share many facility and airfield operations costs with the other DoD-funded activities. As such, it offers the following advantages:

- A site where the economic benefits from the work could help a faltering economy—for example, one with chronically high unemployment—could be selected.

- State and local tax incentives might be available.

_____

[7]NIMA, 2001; U.S. Department of Transportation, 2001.

- JSF noise and environmental issues would be relatively minor additions to an active DoD flying operation.

- The costs of operating the airfield, security, etc., could be shared with DoD activities or organizations already there.

- With little construction required, schedule risk to JSF could be minimized.

Disadvantages associated with this option include the following:

- It does not reduce overcapacity in the military aircraft manufacturing industry.

- It would require different management structures for the DoD activities and JSF FACO activity, so overhead cost avoidance would be small.

- The number of sites available for this option is unknown and would require a site survey of each location to determine its capacity.

- Recruiting FACO production workers should be easier near existing aerospace activities.

Option 5: Selecting a Site with a Current Military Aircraft Production Line That Has Sufficient Capacity to Accommodate JSF FACO Operations

Although this option yields the fewest FACO candidate sites, it also provides the greatest direct savings or cost avoidance to the JSF and other DoD production or maintenance programs. Approximately 20 locations in CONUS have either new production lines or heavy maintenance activity for military aircraft. This option will reduce FACO overhead costs. If the FACO workload is put at existing locations, overhead costs (especially those related to contractor management organization), facilities, security, airfield operation, etc., can be shared with other programs. In addition, taking advantage of the existing contractor management organization may lower some direct costs.

In addition, other advantages include the following:

- Although more limited than previous options, the site with the weakest economy—for example, one with the highest unemployment rate—could be selected.

- It uses some of the overcapacity in military aircraft production.

- It avoids the requirement for other than minor construction of facilities, thereby avoiding costs and schedule risk to the program.

- It should limit the number of new environmental or noise issues at the location.

- It uses the expertise of contractor employees already on site, including production workers, engineers, and managers.

- Much of the cost of a FACO operation stems from overhead costs. Performing FACO at a location with other DoD business would allow the sharing of overhead costs over a wide range of products and cut costs for both the JSF and other military programs.

- It allows the use of the existing DoD plant representative organization at the location.

- Recruiting FACO production workers should be easier near existing aerospace activities.

However, with the number of such sites limited, some of the disadvantages of this option are the following:

- It may conflict with current and planned production at a site in terms of facility asset utilization and schedules.

- State or local tax incentives might be limited at candidate sites compared with other locations.

OPTION AND SITES CHOSEN FOR ANALYSIS

Based on the pros and cons identified above for each of the five options, RAND judges that it would be most cost-effective to choose option 5 for in-depth analysis. While the numerical magnitude of the costs and benefits associated with all these options could not be explicitly assessed, an examination of the construction and administrative tasks associated with the first four options supports that reduction in candidate categories for further study.

Within option 5, RAND assessed the following four locations for in-depth analysis: Lockheed Martin's plant at Fort Worth; Lockheed Martin's plant at Marietta; Lockheed Martin's plant at Palmdale; and Northrop Grumman Air Combat System's leased sites Three and Four at Palmdale. All four locations are run by members of the Lockheed Martin JSF Team. We did not assess locations operated by firms not already associated with JSF, as we will discuss below.

The selected sites meet the basic plant and facilities (excluding tooling) requirements for FACO, with some additions (see Table 3.1). Each site would require some investments. For example, for a split production approach, it would cost $27–65 million to bring any of the three alternative sites up to FACO requirements. This is on top of the approximately $14 million that would be needed at Fort Worth for post-SDD investments for its remaining portion of the work. The costs of these individual site requirements are included in the RAND cost model.

The sponsors of this project directed RAND to analyze Lockheed Martin Team options because to do otherwise would be to diverge from the long-standing JSF winner-take-all strategy, which was reaffirmed as recently as 2001.[8]

Although option 5 could be modified to include a situation where the Lockheed Martin Team could subcontract some of the FACO activity, this would be a unique practice in recent military aircraft experience. Estimating costs associated with it would be problematic because no recent, large-scale experience with aircraft FACO subcontracting has occurred, and thus no relevant precedents exist. Even if other plants were included in this option, it would be difficult to assess the numerous uncertain or unknown costs. These could include payments to Lockheed Martin to share intellectual property for the FACO activities occurring at other companies' locations. The scope

---

[8]Birkler et al., 2001.

of the study did not include an investigation into what kinds of data would have to be shared with an outside firm or how and whether this could effectively be done. This study also did not investigate potential contracting vehicles that would be required to get the Lockheed Martin Team to share proprietary design and production data with outside, non-JSF firms. Further, the issue of warranties on work completed would also have to be negotiated between parties.

Table 3.1

Facilities Requirements for JSF FACO

	Lockheed Martin– Fort Worth[a]	Lockheed Martin– Marietta[b]	Lockheed Martin– Palmdale	Northrop Grumman– Palmdale
8,000-ft runway	Y	Y	Y	Y
FAA instrument approach	Y	Y	Y	Y
Arresting gear	Y	Y	N	N
Taxiways and ramp space	Y	Y	Y	Y
Building (130,000 sq ft)	Y	Y	Y	Y
Air conditioned	Y	Y	N	Y
Paint facility	P[c]	P	N	P[d]
Low-observable building or space	Y	Y	N	N
Flight operations run building	Y	P	N	Y
Hover pad	Y	N	N	N
Road access	Y	Y	Y	Y
Adequate electric power	Y	Y	Y	Y

KEY: Y = present, N = not present, P = partial.

[a]The Fort Worth facilities assessment is after JSF SDD facilitization.

[b]The Marietta facilities assessment assumes use of F-22 production facilities where possible after that program finishes, for example, painting, low-observable testing, flight operations run stations; additional requirements are added to these capabilities at Marietta where needed. Some overlap in 2011 and 2012 between F-22 and JSF production would have to be resolved, depending on the strategy chosen.

[c]"Partial" means some of the required capability is present or will be present when JSF production begins.

[d]Some overlap with B-2 building use will have to be resolved if Site 4 were used as an alternative location.

NOTE: Specific tooling and equipment requirements are listed in Chapter Nine.

CONCLUSION

In terms of alternate locations to the current JSF plan of having all FACO at the Fort Worth plant, any of the other three sites assessed are viable candidates in terms of new facility costs, schedule risk, and retention of the overall JSF winner-take-all strategy. For comparison purposes, the difference in *facility investments only* between performing all FACO at Fort Worth and performing half at Fort Worth and half at one of the other three locations ranges from a savings of about $15–20 million to an additional investment of a little more than $30 million over the base case of 100-percent FACO at Fort Worth (in FY 2002 dollars; these numbers are based on our analysis, which will be discussed later). This equates to a difference for the 3,002 aircraft buy of saving between about $5,000 per aircraft and adding about $10,000 per aircraft for new facilities costs only. The savings in facilities costs will result if part of JSF FACO activities are moved to Marietta after the F-22 goes out of production. However, these facility cost differentials must be factored into the total cost calculations for nonrecurring and recurring costs at varying production rates at the four sites, as will be described in the cost model results covered in Chapter Ten.

Chapter Four

JSF WORKFORCE ISSUES

WORKFORCE ISSUES

An important economic factor in the decision to split FACO operations among different sites is the availability and cost of workers with the requisite skills. Variations in costs at different locations may be a function not only of different basic wage rates but also of hiring and training costs, mandated benefits that differ by location, and various incentives that states might have to encourage new hiring by employers. Multiple FACO locations might also require the relocation of personnel from the base SDD site, Fort Worth, and moving costs would depend on the location of the new site.

In this chapter, we first discuss manufacturing labor in general and the types of labor specifically involved during the JSF FACO process. We also discuss issues of labor cost and availability, including factors besides wages that can affect the overall cost of labor if more than one FACO site is used. We used contractor data on labor costs and other issues and, where possible, collected data from independent sources to confirm it or gain more insight.

LABOR

Manufacturing labor generally falls into two broad categories: direct manufacturing labor and indirect labor. According to the *Defense Acquisition Deskbook*, direct manufacturing labor can be defined as either touch labor or other direct labor. Touch labor is further subdivided into such categories as fabrication, assembly, or test and evaluation. Determination of direct labor costs in general and touch labor costs in particular is important during program development because it in large part drives any estimate of how much a weapon system will cost. The *Defense Acquisition Deskbook* summarizes this issue as follows:

> Contractor-proposed direct labor estimates typically are the foundation of a contractor's cost. Normally, it is the basis on which supporting effort is factored and indirect burden allocated. Therefore, the analysis of direct labor represents an important element of the Production Engineering effort. A large part of the evaluation effort is normally applied to analyzing touch labor requirements. The reason is that touch labor is both the easiest major labor category to evaluate and usually the most important one in terms of actually manufacturing an end item or system. Furthermore, evaluation of touch labor can provide insight into not only the efficient use of labor but also material and manufacturing facilities.[1]

To compare the availability of labor and the costs of FACO operations at different locations, we first determined the FACO tasks required, the labor skills needed for the tasks, the number of hours by skill to accomplish the tasks, and the hourly wages for individuals performing the tasks. With this understanding of JSF labor requirements, we could use the Standard Occupational Classification (SOC) codes developed by the Bureau of Labor Statistics to compare availability and wages at different sites.

LABOR SKILLS FOR THE JSF

Table 4.1 shows the distribution of touch labor skills for F-16 mate-through-delivery in 2001.[2] Lockheed Martin indicates that the distribution for the JSF will be similar.

---

[1]From information provided by HQ AFMC/ENPM on the *Defense Acquisition Deskbook* Web site at http://web2.deskbook.osd.mil.

[2]This information was useful for investigating labor rates. In the cost model, labor hours by FACO function are more important.

Table 4.1

Touch Labor Skill Distribution for
F-16 Mate-Through-Delivery

Touch Labor Category	Percentage of Workers
Painter–finisher	9
Aircraft assembler	40
Aircraft mechanic	13
Avionics technician	10
Electronic repair technician	2
Field and service mechanic	26

Other direct labor categories normally include such functions as material handling, manufacturing engineering, sustaining engineering, tool engineering, tool manufacturing, and quality control. Information about all of these categories was available for FACO operations.

Whereas "direct labor" generally refers to jobs related to the production of a particular product, "indirect labor" refers to jobs that benefit more than one product or the plant as a whole. For example, facility maintenance at a site where more than one weapon system is produced would constitute indirect labor.[3]

If FACO operations are split among different locations, Lockheed Martin will need to ensure the presence of a sufficient number of trained workers to perform all direct and indirect FACO tasks.

Task Distribution and Total Workforce Size for FACO

Table 4.2 is the percentage breakdown by activities of the 2,129 "standard" touch labor hours required in FACO for the CTOL version of the JSF. Similar tables for different JSF variants allow Lockheed Martin to project total direct labor hours by year over the production life of the aircraft.

---

[3]From information provided by HQ AFMC/ENPM on the *Defense Acquisition Desk-book* Web site at http://web2.deskbook.osd.mil.

Table 4.2

Standard Hourly Breakdown for JSF (CTOL Version)

FACO Activity	Percentage of Standard Hours
Structural mate	4.2
Subsystems mate/tail	4.2
Final assembly/test	33.4
Final finishes	28.6
Field operations	29.6

NOTE: This breakout does not correspond to the cycle time requirements in Table 1.2 because labor hours imperfectly map to total time required for any particular task.

Lockheed Martin also provided projections of total FACO staffing from FY 2006 through FY 2026, which were used in the analysis of FACO. Given a single FACO site, Lockheed expects maximum staffing to occur in 2013, when more than 1,000 direct employees will be involved with FACO—about 60 percent of them as touch labor workers. Using multiple sites for JSF FACO will reduce the total number of workers required at any one site, although *not* in exact proportion to the one-site total, because the efficiencies from learning are not likely to be entirely transferred across sites and because duplicate positions or positions that vary with workload might be required.

Standard Occupational Classification System

The Bureau of Labor Statistics (BLS) maintains the Occupational Employment Statistics program, which produces employment and wage estimates for a wide variety of occupations. The number of people employed and estimates of wages paid to them are available by SOC code for the national and state levels as well as for certain metropolitan areas.[4]

---

[4]The SOC system with 821 detailed occupations, 449 broad occupations, 96 minor groups, and 23 major groups was introduced in 2000. This system is the new standard for all federal statistical agencies that report occupational data. Information about the codes can be found at http://stats.bls.gov/oes/oes_ques.htm (last accessed May 30, 2002).

After discussions with Lockheed Martin and a comparison of negotiated wage rates for 2002, we determined that the appropriate associations of FACO activities with SOC codes are those shown in Table
4.3.

The enumeration of the skills required for FACO functions and the
assignment of appropriate SOC codes to those functions allows the
use of BLS and state employment data to determine the notional
costs and availability of workers at potential FACO locations.

COST OF LABOR

Using BLS data and data from individual states, we obtained hourly
wages by metropolitan statistical area (MSA) or county (as appropriate or available) for each direct labor FACO function at each poten-

Table 4.3

FACO Activities and Associated SOC Codes

Activity	Job Skills	Suggested SOC
Touch Labor		
Structural mate	Aircraft assembler	51-2011
Subsystems mate	Aircraft assembler	51-2011
Final assembly	Aircraft assembler	51-2011
Flight operations	Aircraft mechanic	49-3011
	Avionics technician	49-2091
Manloads/ITLs	Aircraft assembler	51-2011
	Electronics repairer	49-2094
Final coatings	Painter (finish)	51-9122
Manufacturing and field operations[a]		
Support Labor		
Manufacturing engineering	Industrial engineer	17-2112
Tool engineering	Industrial engineer	17-2112
Tool manufacturing	Tool and die maker	51-4111
Quality control	Aircraft assembler	51-2011
Engineering	Aerospace engineer	17-2011
Material inventory control	Aircraft assembler	51-2011

[a]"Manufacturing and field operations" is a blanket category used by Lockheed Martin
to provide an average labor rate for touch labor.

tial FACO site.[5] (Specifics are available in Appendix C.) This information was used as a check for rates provided by Lockheed Martin and was the basis for overall labor cost comparisons of different sites.[6]

While the hourly wages reported for the individual occupations listed in Table 4.3 vary quite a bit, the weighted average of the wages (with weights given by the percentage of hours for the activity) is almost 8-percent higher in Palmdale than in Fort Worth. The weighted average for Marietta is a little more than 0.5-percent higher. Lockheed charges the government the same labor rate regardless of the location of the work, but the rate is based on the average of the costs at each site, so moving work from one site to another will change the rate charged. When more than one Lockheed Martin site is used for FACO, we adjust the direct labor rates to reflect the differences in local wage rates.

OTHER COSTS RELATED TO THE WORKFORCE

In addition to wage rates, several other factors could affect the costs of labor at different FACO locations. Among them are training costs, workers' compensation costs, and costs of special benefits that might be required by local legislation. Costs at different locations can also be reduced by such special incentives as hiring or training credits. Tax incentives may also reduce costs. These are presented in the discussion of state and local incentives in Chapter Six.

Training and Other Costs Related to Special Requirements

Aircraft manufacturing involves a number of specialized abilities, and even newly hired workers are often highly skilled. Nonetheless, some additional training is required for new employees brought on board to perform JSF FACO operations. Training time and costs will

---

[5]Texas state data are found at http://www.twc.state.tx.us/customers/rpm/rpmsub3. html (last accessed May 30, 2002); California data are at http://www.calmis.cahwnet. gov; and Georgia data are at http://www.dol.state.ga.us.

[6]Because of restrictions on how data are reported, some wages are unavailable at the county or MSA level. In these cases, either statewide data were used or reasonable assumptions were made based on comparisons of other wages.

vary by specific job certification requirements, but Lockheed Martin estimates an average of 24 hours of training are required for a new worker, at a cost of about $1,000 per employee. We investigated whether certain aspects of JSF FACO, such as the application of special finishes to enhance the low-observable properties of the JSF, would require special skills that would introduce new training requirements for FACO workers. According to Lockheed Martin management, however, JSF FACO operations do not require special or unusual training beyond what is accomplished for F-16 FACO.

Another issue for the JSF is how other special requirements relating to stealth could add to the cost of the workforce. For example, if the application of some finishes or engineering adjustments involved classified procedures or information, more workers would require background checks to obtain security clearances. Conducting FACO at multiple locations would increase the requirement for cleared workers. Lockheed Martin reported that the FACO assembly line would be structured to limit access to classified areas so that the number of personnel needing clearances would be reduced. But even a line structured to minimize the number of classified workers could still require up to 20 percent of the FACO workers to have clearances (as we also report in Chapter Eight). Both Lockheed Martin's Fort Worth and Marietta facilities have an adequate number of cleared workers who could be transferred to the JSF as their other work declines. Palmdale has a large number of cleared workers employed by both Lockheed Martin and by Northrop Grumman, as well as many others holding clearances from previous aircraft manufacturing experience. At all locations, obtaining sufficient numbers of appropriately cleared workers is considered a manageable task with the necessary lead time for background checks. Hence, finding cleared workers and obtaining clearances is not expected to be an expense that would affect the potential locations differently, and expenses related to them have not been included in the cost analysis.

Workers' Compensation Costs

Another source of labor cost variation is workers' compensation. This cost is included in fringe rates, which are often uniform across sites. The magnitude of these costs is not significant, on the order of a couple hundred dollars a year per employee. For Lockheed Martin, they are about twice as expensive in Palmdale as they are at Fort Worth and Marietta.

Special Costs Related to Different Locations

According to Lockheed Martin, a "9/80" work schedule was implemented at the Fort Worth plant in April 2000. It is available to salaried employees, some represented employees, and contract labor personnel. This schedule allows individuals to adjust their work hours in a two-week period so that they complete 80 hours of work in nine days and have the Friday of the second week as an additional day off. This is an extremely popular benefit among those eligible for it, and there is interest in expanding it to more workers, but Lockheed Martin expressed concern that attempting to do so in California would increase FACO costs. California Assembly Bill No. 60, which took effect in January 2000, requires work done in excess of an 8-hour day or in excess of a 40-hour week to be compensated at a rate of 1.5 times the worker's regular pay.[7] Lockheed Martin estimates that if the 9/80 work schedule were implemented, Bill No. 60 could result in an average of $2,000 in overtime per year for each employee. However, the law allows alternative work schedules, such as 9/80 without overtime payments, if they are approved by two-thirds of the affected workers. According to managers at Palmdale, this approval has been obtained, and the new schedule will apply not only to current employees, but also to any new workers hired. In the event that workers vote to withdraw their approval, the plant would return to a normal schedule with an 8-hour day and 40-hour week.

Costs Related to Mandated Benefits for Employees

Employers might be required to provide certain services either because of state or local legislation or as the result of local labor union agreements. Such services do not appear to be a factor in JSF FACO labor costs. In general, rather than mandating services (such

---

[7]The text of Chapter 134 of the bill can be found at http://www.usc.edu/dept/engineering/efc/issues/pdf/ab_60_bill_19990721_chaptered.pdf (last accessed May 30, 2002).

as child care), states and localities provide tax incentives for providing them.[8]

It is possible that varying union pressure to provide services could affect costs in different locations—Texas and Georgia are "right to work" states, California is not.[9] "Right to work" laws may sometimes be seen as part of a climate that is favorable to business, although it can never be exactly predicted how this climate will affect costs. Lockheed Martin employees are represented by a union at all potential FACO locations, and the Northrop Grumman workers are not. To the extent that this is a factor, it would be reflected in overhead costs.

Hiring and Training Incentive Programs

Some states have legislated incentives for hiring certain types of workers or for providing training (these are covered in detail in Chapter Six). Firms in Antelope Valley, where Palmdale is located, can take advantage of certain hiring tax credits that are applicable to FACO. These credits are included in our analysis. (Other California tax credits applicable to the JSF will phase out before the production process begins.[10]) Texas has no applicable hiring tax credits. Georgia does, but requires firms to choose among the hiring credit and two investment credits. One of the investment credits provided greater savings in our analysis, and hence the hiring tax credit was not included here.

Lockheed Martin estimates that the cost of hiring a new touch labor FACO worker in Fort Worth is on the order of several thousand dollars.[11]

---

[8]See *State Business Incentives*, 2000.

[9]"Right to work" laws mean that employees cannot be required to join unions at their place of work, although even nonunion workers are covered by the contract. This weakens the strength of unions, in part because of reduced financial resources from the collection of fewer union dues.

[10]According to *State Business Incentives* (2000, p. 23), the credits apply to taxpayers "under initial contract or subcontract to manufacture property for ultimate use in the Joint Strike Fighter."

[11]The exact number is incorporated into our cost analysis and is assumed to be the same across all sites.

AVAILABILITY OF WORKERS

We have found that it will be little problem finding workers to perform all FACO activities at any of the sites under consideration. If all work is done in Fort Worth, Lockheed Martin expects to have 4,500 people involved with JSF production there by 2005. This figure would be out of a total of 13,500 employees at the Fort Worth plant and would represent a net increase of about 2,000 jobs over 2001 employment levels.[12] The number of people involved in FACO by 2005, however, is quite small: According to projected staffing estimates, FACO direct labor will require fewer than 200 people in 2005. While direct labor requirements will steadily increase until a peak of about 1,000 in 2013, this period will coincide with the discontinuation of F-16 production in Fort Worth, and many personnel will transfer from one aircraft to the other. Thus, the number of new hires for FACO operations will average fewer than 100 per year.[13] In Marietta, F-22 operations will tail off at about the same time under the current work plan and, therefore, a similar transfer of workers would be possible at that site.

RAND independently checked the availability of workers at potential FACO sites using national employment data from the BLS[14] and data collected by individual states. Our analysis indicates that, given current and projected employment in FACO related occupations, sufficient workers would be available at any of the locations.[15]

---

[12]Richard Whittle, "JSF Would Save Lockheed Jobs," *Dallas Morning News*, August 23, 2001, p. D1. (Lockheed Martin specifically prepared projections for this article.)

[13]Whittle, 2001.

[14]National employment data for 2000 with projections to 2010 can be found at http://www.bls.gov/emp/emptab21.htm (last accessed May 30, 2002). Data are updated every two years. Values for the current year and the projected year are given in this table, but values for intermediate years are not calculated. Data in the table are presented by occupational grouping, but without listing the SOC. Employment data for 1999, which are arranged by SOC, can be found at http://stats.bls.gov/oes/1999/oes_11Ma.htm (last accessed May 30, 2002).

[15]The most current state data includes 1998 employment with projections for 2008. This complicated the study of employment data somewhat because before 2000, OES information was compiled using a different classification system, and the SOC codes in Table 4.3 had to be converted into the old codes to be able to examine employment projections. The National Crosswalk Service Center (at http://www.state.ia.us/ncdc/) has tables that list the new codes that correspond to the old codes.

While these data provide a sense of the availability of appropriate workers as JSF production increases, the assessments of the potential FACO locations should also be considered. Obviously, Lockheed is not concerned about workforce availability in Fort Worth because that is its first choice for JSF production. As part of a 1999 study, the city of Palmdale argued that its resident workforce was more than sufficient for *all* JSF production.[16] Lockheed Martin is the third-largest employer in Cobb County, Ga., with 7,000 employees engaged in aircraft design, development, and production, and a presentation to this study by the Georgia Department of Industry, Trade, and Tourism showed its confidence in the availability of sufficient workers for FACO.[17] Finally, during interviews conducted for another research effort,[18] managers involved with aircraft production in different parts of the country have indicated that jobs with Lockheed Martin and other aircraft prime contractors are sought-after for their relatively high wages and benefits, and thus hiring workers poses few problems.

SUMMARY

To determine the direct labor costs for each of the components of production labor in Table 4.3, the cost analysis multiplies the number of hours of work on a yearly basis at each site by the direct labor rate (the FPRA [Forward Pricing Rate Agreement] rate in 2002). Hiring and training costs are included as described in Chapter Nine.

Although labor is obviously critical to JSF FACO, it is important to note that these costs are relatively insignificant as a percentage of total JSF costs. If Lockheed Martin's estimate that FACO makes up only 2 percent of URF costs holds true, the FACO direct labor component will be something less than that 2 percent. Any local differences in wages and benefits for FACO workers will make only a small contribution to differences in total JSF program costs.

---

[16] *JSF Site Cost-Effectiveness Study,* study conducted by SDS International of Arlington, Va., for the city of Palmdale and the California Trade and Commerce Agency, June 17, 1999.

[17] Information provided to RAND by the Georgia Department of Industry, Trade, and Tourism, October 2001.

[18] Cook and Graser, 2001.

Chapter Five

INDIRECT COSTS

This chapter provides a brief overview of the types of costs involved in producing the JSF for those unfamiliar with how DoD and its contractors determine and allocate costs to defense programs. In particular, the objective is to describe indirect costs and then to describe how these costs might vary across locations and how that variance might affect JSF FACO costs. Indirect costs are an important consideration in the final cost of the JSF because these costs normally constitute more than half the costs incurred at any manufacturing location for DoD systems.

BACKGROUND

Because of the lack of a true commercial marketplace for military aircraft, where other comparable products can be used for price comparisons, the production price paid by DoD for the JSF will be a negotiation between DoD contract administration personnel and those of Lockheed Martin. These negotiations will be largely based on forecast costs derived by government cost and price analysts as well as those of Lockheed Martin. Early in production, estimators will use the actual costs of other aircraft previously built and adjusted for JSF differences and/or the actual costs of producing the JSF SDD aircraft—again, adjusted for differences in content between development and production aircraft. DoD and its contractors for most military-unique products follow this process. Over the years, a complex categorization of the various types of costs involving military production has evolved so that the government and its contractors can use this categorization to expedite the negotiations on final prices for military systems.[1]

The first major division of these costs is into two categories called "direct" and "indirect" costs. Direct costs are those that can be associated directly with the development and/or production of a specific DoD system, including such items as direct labor (engineering, tooling, manufacturing, etc.) and direct materials (which may range from unprocessed basic materials to complete assemblies). The viewpoint taken in this report is from the prime contractor's perspective, but each intermediate manufacturer goes through the same categorization when it converts material into final products, which may be subassemblies for use in the next higher level of manufacturing. Direct costs are accounted for and tracked in the contractor's accounting system to a specific system being developed or manufactured for DoD.

Indirect costs are those not easily identifiable with a specific system or those that, because they represent relatively small sums, may not justify separate tracking to a specific system. These indirect costs are generally further subdivided into two major categories: overhead costs and general and administrative (G&A) expenses. Overhead costs are those that are indirectly related to an area of development or production and include such items as electrical power; depreciation; heating, ventilation, and air conditioning (HVAC); computer services; and employee fringe benefits. Corporations often further subdivide overhead into areas identifiable to a function—engineering overhead, manufacturing overhead, etc. G&A expenses cover activities related more to the overall functioning of the corporation, with little identifiable relationship to specific development or manufacturing operations. Included in G&A are the salaries of corporate officers, the cost of operating a corporate headquarters, independent research and development, and bid and proposal costs. This discussion implies that the division between the various cost categories would be the same with all DoD contractors; but in reality this categorization varies somewhat among DoD contractors, between sites

---

[1]Two excellent sources of information on the categorization of DoD costs are *Indirect-Cost Management Guide: Navigating the Sea of Overhead* by the Defense Systems Management College (DSMC) and the Defense Acquisition Deskbook at http://web1.deskbook.osd.mil.

of the same contractor, and even at the same location over time—so direct comparisons of these costs is difficult at best.

If one company were developing and manufacturing only one DoD system at one location, all costs could be considered direct costs because any costs incurred by that company would be directly related to that system. Thus, whether a cost is direct or indirect would be a theoretical discussion because all costs could be billed to that one program. Such a case is rare because most contractors develop and produce several DoD systems at more than one location or may produce both military and commercial systems or may produce items for Foreign Military Sales. One might ask whether it would be easier for DoD to just pay the costs annually at specific locations where only DoD-related activity took place, rather than going through a complex cost determination and allocation process. Many arguments could be offered for keeping the current allocation process, but the strongest is that it provides the best visibility into the individual costs of various DoD programs so that senior decision-makers and Congress have the most accurate cost information related to DoD programs.

Because indirect costs are not readily identifiable with a specific product, some system of allocating these costs among DoD programs, as well as to commercial programs, is required. This is an important issue because indirect costs are normally larger than the direct costs incurred at a manufacturing plant. The first step in developing an allocation scheme is to organize the indirect costs into cost "pools," which relate to the direct function supported. For example, all indirect costs forecast to be incurred by a company related to its manufacturing function would be categorized into a manufacturing cost pool. Next, some basis of allocation among programs is determined. The most commonly used allocation method is one related to a direct expense, such as direct labor hours. The total overhead costs divided by the basis of allocation produces an overhead rate. Thus, if a company forecasts it will incur $100 million annually in the manufacturing overhead account and also forecasts that it will use 1 million manufacturing hours, the manufacturing overhead rate would be $100 per hour. If a specific program were projected to use 250,000 manufacturing hours, it would be billed for $25 million of overhead costs.

Indirect costs have a fixed and variable component. The fixed part of these costs does not change over the short run. For example, depreciation on a plant would not change whether the production activity were relatively high or low because depreciation is normally based on the original cost and the passage of time. The variable part of overhead costs changes by activity level. An example of this might be employee fringe benefits or electrical power consumption. With high production output, increased fringe benefit costs would result from larger numbers of employees working on the program, or greater usage of machines and test equipment would result in higher electrical consumption. By their nature, indirect costs tend to have a larger fixed component compared with the variable portion. These costs vary by location, not only in the magnitude of the total, but also the fixed and variable components.

Annually, DoD auditors and contract administrators go through a process to develop FPRAs, which involve detailed analyses of direct and indirect costs incurred in the past and forecast to be incurred in the future. FPRAs are expressed in terms of a dollars-per-allocation basis—again, normally direct labor hours. These rates are often termed "wrap" rates because an hour of labor used to produce a DoD system would include the wages of the worker, the overhead costs of supporting the worker, and an element of the G&A expense. The total number of units in the basis of allocation (direct labor hours or some other factor) at a facility is often termed the "business base" to reflect the level of activity at a location. Generally, several rates reflect the different direct cost activities; therefore, a location might have an engineering rate, a tooling rate, a manufacturing rate, etc.

Because the indirect costs have a large fixed component, one way to minimize the costs of a program is to produce the greatest number of goods possible at a specific location (maximize its business base), thus spreading the overhead costs over as many systems or units as possible. In the defense industry today, production rates are low compared with capacity. DoD is continually pressuring defense contractors to lower their overhead costs to keep the FPRAs under control, in some cases by closing facilities. Few, if any, locations in the United States producing DoD systems are anywhere near maximum production capacity. (One might take this argument to its logical extreme and ask whether DoD should require its defense contractors to produce all of their work at a single site. However, "diseconomies of scale" may arise. These occur when the sheer size of the facility and amount of work performed there become too large to be properly managed.)

EFFECT OF INDIRECT COSTS ON JSF FACO LOCATION

A prime objective of this study is to determine what the costs to DoD would be if the business base resulting from FACO activities were spread to more than one location. At the first level of analysis, it seems that the rates at Fort Worth would increase because the same fixed costs would be spread over a smaller business base if some JSF business base were moved elsewhere. This would increase the cost of the JSFs assembled at Fort Worth, as well as increase the costs of other DoD programs at the facility. Theoretically, if some portion of FACO were moved out of the Fort Worth plant, the FPRAs would rise because the indirect costs would have to be covered by less direct activity. However, if the FACO business base were moved to another Lockheed Martin location where DoD programs were being conducted, the FPRAs at that location(s) should be reduced due to the addition of the JSF FACO business base. Thus, the DoD programs manufactured at either (or both) Palmdale or Marietta could be decreased by such a movement of business base. This reduction would be at least partially offset by added overhead costs at Palmdale or Marietta for such costs as new facilities, equipment, and environmental compliance costs. New site overhead rates would be calculated as follows:

$$\frac{\text{existing overhead costs} + \text{additional FACO overhead costs}}{\text{existing business base} + \text{FACO business base.}}$$

One of the key questions in the analysis of creation of more than one FACO site is whether moving some or all of the FACO business base from the Lockheed Martin Fort Worth plant to another DoD production location would change the total cost of JSF FACO and the total costs of other DoD programs. In other words, would the negative effect on the rates and DoD programs at Fort Worth by reducing FACO activity be offset by the positive effect on the rates and programs by increasing activity at another Lockheed Martin location? As the analysis in Chapter Ten will show, moving the FACO activity from Fort Worth has a tangible effect on total overhead costs.

RAND has investigated the overhead rates at the four potential locations, gathering as much specific data as possible. Specifics are not releasable because overhead rates are proprietary to the companies. The link between FACO activities and overhead rates at the different sites has been incorporated into the model. Thus, the RAND analysis estimates the total impact on all DoD programs (including JSF) at Fort Worth and alternative sites by incorporating the puts and takes of this business base at the sites by adjusting forecast rates at each location under several production scenarios. This analysis provides a more accurate assessment of JSF FACO options in terms of the total DoD costs involved (see Chapter Ten for details).

Chapter Six

STATE AND LOCAL TAX CREDITS AND INCENTIVES

When making the decision on where to locate production activities, firms often consider state tax credits and state and local incentives. This chapter addresses these economic development activities, along with a discussion of state and local taxes. Because tax credits and incentives are generally taken as reductions to tax liabilities, they must be understood in the context of the broader tax climate of the location. We briefly discuss the historical use of tax credits and incentives to set the stage for the discussion of these issues with particular reference to JSF FACO.

Also in this chapter, we describe the specific tax and business incentives that would affect the costs of JSF FACO in Texas, California, and Georgia. We collected data from a number of sources in support of this analysis and gathered the tax information and program descriptions from the economic development offices in these states, from state Web sites, and from published sources. We also contacted Lockheed Martin and Northrop Grumman and local DCMA offices to learn about participation in these programs.

Tables 6.1–6.3 summarize the major taxes and incentive programs that would apply to FACO at the three potential locations of Fort Worth, Marietta, and Palmdale. The applicable tax liabilities and savings from economic development programs are incorporated into RAND cost estimates.

Table 6.1
State Taxes and Their Impact on JSF FACO

Type of Tax	Basis of Application	California Rate	Applicable to JSF?	Georgia Rate	Applicable to JSF?	Texas Rate	Applicable to JSF?
State/local sales taxes on real property	Purchase price	None	No	None	No	None	No
State/local property taxes on real property	Assessed value[a]	1.10% annually on 100% of assessed value	Yes[b]	Effective rate of 1.201% annually on 100% of assessed value	No: AFP 6 real property is not taxed	2.64% annually on 100% of assessed value	None/exempt
State/local sales/use taxes on facilities, tooling, and equipment (contractor-owned)[c]	Purchase price	8.25% at the time of purchase	Yes	5% at time of purchase	No[d]	8.25% at time of purchase	No[d]
State/local sales/use taxes on facilities, tooling and equipment (government-owned)	Purchase price	8.25% at the time of purchase	No[e]	5% at time of purchase	No[e]	8.25% at time of purchase	No[e]
State/local property taxes on facilities, tooling, and equipment (contractor-owned)	Assessed value[a]	1.10% annually	Yes	1.201% annually	Yes	2.64% annually	Yes

Table 6.1—continued

Type of Tax	Basis of Application	California Rate	Applicable to JSF?	Georgia Rate	Applicable to JSF?	Texas Rate	Applicable to JSF?
State/local property taxes on facilities, tooling, and equipment (government-owned)	Assessed value[a]	1.10% annually	Yes[b,e]	1.201% annually	No[e]	2.64% annually	No[e]
State/local sales/use taxes on raw material, purchased parts, and subassemblies	Purchase price	8.25% at time of purchase	No[e,f]	5% at time of purchase	No[e,f]	8.25% at time of purchase	No[e,f]
Property taxes on raw material, purchased parts, and subassemblies	Purchase price[a]	1.1% annually	No[e]	1.201% annually	No[e]	2.64% annually	No[e]
State/local sales tax on JSF sales to DoD	Sales price	8.25%	No[g]	5%	No[g]	8.25%	No[g]
Corporate franchise/income taxes on JSF sales	Net income (sales price minus all costs)	8.84%	Yes	6%	Yes	4.50%	Yes[h]

[a] For the purposes of modeling, this was assumed to be net book value.

[b] Although real property (land and improvements) located on government-owned facilities is normally not subject to property taxes, California taxes the "possessory interest" (value of the property) at the property tax rate.

[c] Handtools, office furniture, and equipment are already included in overhead rates and therefore taxes on these items are not included in the model.

[d] FACO purchases are exempt because—in Georgia and Texas—manufacturing machinery and equipment is exempt from state and local taxes.

[e] DoD will fund and retain title to the JSF tooling and equipment, parts, and subassemblies before use; therefore, it is not subject to state and local taxes.

[f] If sales taxes are applied on raw materials, they are already included in costs to the company.

[g] DoD is exempt from paying state or local sales taxes on purchases.

[h] Texas taxes corporations at the higher of either 0.25 percent of net taxable capital or on 4.5 percent of net income derived in Texas.

Table 6.2
California Tax Credits and Incentives

Credit or Incentive	Basis of Application	Applicable to JSF FACO?	Credit/Incentive	Comments
Manufacturing investment credit on manufacturing equipment and special-use aerospace buildings	Offset to California franchise (state income) tax liability	Yes	6% of purchase price and capitalized labor can be applied against California franchise (state income) tax liability	Limited to maximum of tax liability, may be carried over for eight years
Research and development credits	Offset to California franchise (state income) tax liability	No	11% of in-house costs; 24% for purchased efforts	JSF research and development to be accomplished in SDD phase in Fort Worth
JSF wage tax credit (expires in 2005)	Offset to California franchise (state income) tax liability	Yes (but credit will expire before FACO activities begin)	Percentage (50–10% declining, 10% annually from 2001–2006) of qualified wages (direct labor costs) not to exceed $10,000 per worker per year	Not applied in RAND cost model because it will expire
JSF property tax credit (expires in 2005)	Offset to California franchise (state income) tax liability	Yes (but credit will expire before FACO activities begin)	10% of the cost of qualified property (used 50% of the time or more in activities to manufacture the JSF)	Not applied in RAND cost model because it will expire

Table 6.2—continued

Credit or Incentive	Basis of Application	Applicable to JSF FACO?	Credit/Incentive	Comments
Enterprise Zone Incentives				
State hiring tax credit	Offset to California franchise (state income) tax liability	Yes	$31,590 over first five years[a]	Experience at Palmdale indicates that about 20% of the hired workers qualify
Business equipment, furniture, and fixtures deduction	Deduction in year of purchase against revenue in calculating California franchise (state income) tax liability	Yes	40% of purchase price not to exceed $20,000 annually (onetime expense for each piece of equipment)	Cannot be applied unless sales/use tax was paid on purchase; property may also be depreciated in subsequent years
Net operating loss carryover	Offset to California franchise (state income) tax liability	Yes	Total offset against tax liability	Not applied in RAND cost model because information on California losses not available
State sales and use tax credit	Offset to California franchise (state income) tax liability	Yes	8% of purchase price, plus capitalized labor	First $20 million of purchases eligible for credit ($1.6 million maximum)

[a]Credit is based on 50 percent of 150 percent of qualified wages (maximum of $6.75 per hour or minimum wage) for first year and declines to 40/30/20/10 percent, respectively, in next four successive years.

Table 6.3
Georgia Tax Credits and Incentives

Georgia Tier 4 Credits and Incentives[a]	Basis of Application	Applicable to JSF?	Credit/Incentive	Comments
Job tax credit	Offset to state income tax liability	Yes	$750 per job annually for five years following creation of the job	Limited to 50% of tax liability per year
Investment tax credit	Offset to state income tax liability	Yes	1% credit for each $50,000 investment (onetime); 3% for recycling, pollution control, and defense conversions	Only one of these three Georgia credits may be taken—this was the one used in the model
Optional investment tax credit	Offset to state income tax liability	Yes	See text for explanation	

[a]Companies may only participate in one of these three programs.

STATE AND LOCAL ECONOMIC DEVELOPMENT

State and local governments regularly provide customized assistance to individual firms. Over the past 30 years, every state and almost all metropolitan areas have expanded the size and scope of economic development programs—i.e., those meant to induce businesses to locate (or remain) in their state or locality. Bartik (1991) describes three waves in this expansion. The first wave, occurring in the 1950s–1970s, included mainly financial assistance, such as tax relief or subsidizing business research. Before the 1970s, U.S. state and local governments, particularly in the South, developed financial programs to aggressively recruit manufacturing branch plants from the North.

Recessions and industrial restructuring during the 1970s and 1980s led states, during the second wave, to a significant expansion of financial programs and included nonfinancial incentives to start-up businesses, small businesses, and existing businesses. State and local governments cut back on many of these programs because of budgetary shortfalls from the 1990–1991 recession. In addition, critics of development programs argued that little evidence of the effectiveness of state and local economic development programs could be found, in part because these programs only directly benefited a relatively small number of businesses.

The third wave, in the 1990s, saw state and local governments outsourcing many development activities. Rather than having governments pay 100 percent of the costs of providing services to selected businesses, private or quasiprivate companies provided economic development with state or local governments' guidance and subsidies.

Effectiveness of Development Programs

Today, state and local governments use these programs to compete with other states or localities for increased jobs in their jurisdictions. More jobs are expected to bring such benefits as lower local unemployment and increased wages, property values, profits for local businesses, and tax revenues—and reelection for the politicians who successfully attract new businesses.

The traditional economic view of state and local economic development programs is that, at best, they have no national benefit and, at worst, they are contrary to the national interest.[1] There are three parts to this argument. First, from a national perspective, state and local economic development programs are thought to be a zero-sum game: one area's benefits from gaining jobs are matched by another area's costs from losing jobs. Second, more locally, the programs have little effect on the growth of a small region because state and local taxes are too small a percentage of business costs to affect business growth decisions, especially because these taxes are deductible from federal income tax. Third and most important, competition for jobs may lead to a "race to the bottom" that worsens the income distribution by lowering business-tax revenue and public expenditure levels.

Not all economists agree with the standard view. For example, Brennan and Buchanan (1980) suggest that the total size of government would be excessive in the absence of intergovernmental tax competition. More recently, Bartik (1991) argues that economic development can provide benefits, although these may not greatly outweigh the costs. Programs are not zero-sum if they provide jobs in depressed areas, where new jobs add most to overall national economic welfare. Bartik also points out that even small production cost differentials could be decisive in business location decisions if states and metropolitan areas are close substitutes.

STATE AND LOCAL TAXES IN CALIFORNIA, GEORGIA, AND TEXAS

Each state has a unique combination of tax instruments that vary by rates, bases, and—given that local governments may also tax businesses—by locality. State governments typically tax a portion of corporate net income based on the presence of that firm in the state. Local governments typically tax sales and property in their jurisdictions. In some states, property is also taxed at the state level.

To assess the impact of taxes on different FACO strategies, we examined the state and local tax rates and bases at the three potential

---

[1] See, for example, Oates, 1972; Zodrow and Mieszkowski, 1986; and Wilson, 1986.

FACO locations. Major taxes affecting FACO would be the state corporate income or franchise tax, state and local sales and use tax, and state and local property tax.[2] A summary of the relevant taxes for the three states is presented in Table 6.1.

State Franchise and Corporate Income Taxes

Generally, states tax net income earned in that state. The rules for determining taxable income base vary by state according to apportionment formulas that, for companies operating in more than one state, determine income earned in that state and state-specific deductions for business expenses and credits. Table 6.1 shows the state franchise tax rates for California, Georgia, and Texas. Corporations in Texas are taxed the greater of 0.25 percent of net taxable capital and 4.5 percent of net income derived in Texas.[3] (In most years, Lockheed Martin has paid Texas franchise taxes according to the net income calculation.) Georgia's corporate income tax rate is slightly higher, at 6 percent, while California has the highest franchise taxes of the three states, at 8.84 percent.

Property Taxes

States and localities may impose taxes on the assessed value of real and tangible "personal" property.[4] Property taxes are determined by tax rates and assessment values that vary by location. In general, business personal property, such as machinery, equipment, and inventory, are assessed according to cost less depreciation. The value of real property, such as land and buildings, is determined by local appraisers according to the sales of comparable properties.[5] Because we do not have data on comparable property, we assume that the taxable value for property for FACO is the cost less depreciation.

---

[2]The employer's share of workers' compensation is included in the fringe rates.

[3]Taxable capital is a corporation's state capital (capital stock) plus surplus. Surplus means the net assets of the company minus its members' contributions.

[4]Businesses face tangible "personal" property taxes for all property that is not "real" property, which includes land and improvements to land.

[5]In California, growth in assessments is limited to 2 percent per year.

Texas has no state property tax. Furthermore, because the Lockheed Martin site in Fort Worth is in a federal enclave within AFP 4, it is exempt from local property taxes on its equipment. In California, the property tax is effectively a statewide tax.[6] The state, city, county, and school districts all tax property in Georgia. Each government entity uses a different tax rate and assessment ratio. Table 6.1 reports the tax rates for each locality.

AFP 4 in Texas is exempt from property taxes. Property in Marietta is taxed at an effective rate $12.01 per $1,000 or 1.201 percent of assessed market value. However, real property on AFP 6 is exempt from Georgia property taxes. Property at the Palmdale location is taxed at 1.1 percent of assessed market value. In most states, like Texas and Georgia, the property for FACO activities that would be located on government-owned plants would not be subject to property taxes. However, California taxes the "possessory interests," the value of government-owned property that is used by contractors. The tax rate and base are the same as if the property were privately owned. As will be discussed in the description of the cost analysis in Chapter Nine, property taxes on existing, privately owned property are already included in the overhead and are therefore addressed in the base rates in the cost model. Property taxes on new property for FACO are included in the calculation of the new effective overhead rates.

Sales and Use Taxes

Although sales taxes are collected at the time of purchase on goods and services, these taxes are not assessed on goods for which the title is passed to the government before use. Our analysis assumes that all manufacturing tooling and equipment purchased exclusively for the JSF will be owned by DoD and not subject to sales or use taxes. Therefore, these items are not eligible for sales or investment tax credits.[7] There may be some non-JSF-specific facilities, tooling, and

---

[6]Voters in local communities can increase property taxes with a two-thirds majority override referendum.

[7]Sales taxes are applied to gross receipts from retail sales of tangible personal property. Use taxes complement sales taxes. They are applied at the same rate as the sales tax for goods and services not subject to the sales tax, such as out-of-state or Internet

equipment purchased for FACO that could be used in nongovernmental programs. These items would be subject to sales or use taxes (as well as property taxes) and would be contractor-owned. However, these could qualify for tax credits.

TAX CREDITS AND DEDUCTIONS

State taxes cannot be evaluated alone without understanding the state tax benefits and state and local incentives offered to attract business. Generally, these are taken as a reduction in taxes, so merely looking at the tax rates fails to provide a complete picture of these costs of doing business.

State and Local Economic Development Programs

All three states use development programs to a greater or lesser extent to recruit businesses to relocate or expand in their jurisdiction. The states offer both tax credits and business incentives to firms in general; in specific industries, such as manufacturing; and in regions or enterprise zones. Of the three states, Texas offers the least-extensive tax credits and incentives applicable to JSF FACO activities, while California has the most generous package.

Texas

Limited development programs are available to Lockheed Martin in Texas. Most of the incentive programs in Texas are targeted to encourage development in rural areas, strategic investment areas, or enterprise zones. The Fort Worth site is not eligible for many franchise tax credits because it is not in these targeted areas. Texas established franchise tax credits for research and development conducted anywhere in the state. However, little research relating to FACO is expected during the production phase of the JSF program. Thus, these credits would not apply to FACO activities under study here.

---

purchases. Total state and local sales taxes are 8.25 percent in Palmdale, 5.00 percent in Marietta, and 8.25 percent in Fort Worth.

The Fort Worth site is in a federal enclave and is exempt from the local property taxes (the current local property tax rate for Tarrant County is $2.64 per $100). Thus, our model does not include any property tax liability for Lockheed Martin in Texas. Manufacturing equipment is exempt from sales and use tax in Texas.

Georgia

Georgia directs economic development toward counties in most need of economic growth. To determine need, the state ranks counties and census tracts into four economic tiers according to the unemployment rate, per-capita income, and percentage of residents below the poverty level. The Lockheed Martin–Marietta site is in Cobb County, which is ranked as a Tier 4 county. Counties with this ranking have the lowest unemployment rates, fewest poor residents, and highest per-capita income.

Tier 4 Credits. *Job Tax Credit.* Firms may reduce franchise taxes by $750 for each new job created if the jobs total 25 or more and the new jobs are held by residents in Cobb County. Credits are allowed for new full-time employee jobs for five years in years two through six following the creation of the jobs. In Tier 4 counties, the total credit amount may offset up to 50 percent of the state income tax liability in a taxable year.

Investment Tax Credit. This credit is based on the same tiers as the job tax credit program. The program allows existing manufacturing to obtain a credit against corporate income tax liability. Companies in Cobb County must invest $50,000 to receive a 1-percent tax credit. The credit increases to 3 percent for recycling, pollution control, and defense conversion activities.

Optional Investment Tax Credit. Firms in Cobb County that qualify for the investment tax credit and invest at least $20 million may choose this credit instead. The credit may be claimed for 10 years, provided the qualifying property remains in service throughout that period. The credit is calculated based on a three-year tax liability average. The annual credits are then determined using this base-year average. The credit available to the taxpayer in any given year is the minimum of: (1) the 90 percent of the increase in tax liability in the current taxable year over that in the base year; or (2) the excess of the aggregate amount of the credit allowed over the sum of the amounts of credit already used in the years following the base year.

Limitations. Firms may only take advantage of one of these three programs. According to our analysis, the investment tax credit is likely to yield the largest savings. Hence, it is included in the cost analysis.

Manufacturing Machinery and Computer Sales Tax Exemption. These are exempt from sales and use tax in Georgia.

California

The California legislature offers an aggressive set of tax credit and business incentive programs to attract firms involved in aerospace manufacturing.[8] This includes the statewide Manufacturers' Investment Credit, Research and Development Credits, and Enterprise Zone programs. There are also tax credits directed specifically to the JSF, but these will expire before the production phase of the program starts, and are not expected to be renewed.

Antelope Valley Enterprise Zone Development Programs. California's enterprise zone programs allow companies that are within any of the 39 designated zones incentives and programs not available to businesses outside of the zones. The Lockheed Martin and Northrop Grumman sites at Palmdale are located in the Antelope Valley Enterprise Zone (AVEZ) and would be eligible for many of the programs. The AVEZ was created in 1997 for a 15-year period, and thus would expire in 2012—in the middle of JSF FACO. The legislation allows for a single five-year extension if certain qualifications are met. The California legislature is considering extending these enterprise zone programs by five years for a total of 20 years. Given this history, we assume the enterprise zone will be renewed and therefore include these credits in our analysis up to 2017.

---

[8]In a 1999 report, the city of Palmdale and the California Trade and Commerce Agency investigated the cost savings from California's economic development programs. This study reported substantial program savings, but did not report on tax liabilities in California. Most of the programs would not apply to production (City of Palmdale and the California Trade and Commerce Agency, 1999).

State Hiring Tax Credit. Firms located in the AVEZ may reduce franchise taxes by a proportion of annual wage costs per qualified worker for the first 60 months that the worker is on the job. Qualified workers must

- Spend at least 90 percent of their time on activities related to businesses within the AVEZ

- Perform at least 50 percent of the work within the AVEZ

- When hired, fall into one of several targeted groups of workers, including veterans, displaced workers from military installation closures, and certain other unemployed workers.

The credit is a percentage of the smaller of the actual hourly wage paid or 150 percent of the minimum wage, which is $6.75 an hour. Actual wages paid to aircraft workers far exceed 150 percent of the minimum wage, so the amount based on the minimum wage would apply. The credit starts at 50 percent of the qualified wages, and declines to 40 percent the second year, 30 percent in the third year, 20 percent in the fourth year, 10 percent in the fifth year, and then disappears. Assuming no change in the minimum wage, the maximum benefit per worker would total $31,590 over five years. RAND received three estimates of the number of workers that would qualify for this credit. We used the average, 20 percent (which also was the median number) for both companies operating in Palmdale.

Business Expense Deductions. All firms in the AVEZ can deduct the cost of qualifying business equipment, furniture, and fixtures (or other depreciable personal property) as a business expense in the year they are placed into service. The maximum deduction is the lesser of 40 percent of the cost of the qualified property or $20,000 per year. We assume the maximum deduction of $20,000 per year. Property must be used within the enterprise zone.

Net Operating Loss Carryover. Firms in the AVEZ may carry 50 percent of a loss forward from one tax year to the next to offset income in the following years. As it is difficult to predict future business losses, no credit for this program is given in our analysis.

Other Major Statewide Development Programs. *Manufacturing Investment Credit.* The Manufacturing Investment Credit (MIC) is a credit that can reduce a company's California franchise taxes. This credit allows all manufacturers to deduct 6 percent of manufacturing equipment costs and also allows aerospace manufacturers to extend the credit to special-purpose buildings and foundation costs and capitalized labor costs that are directly applicable to the construction of manufacturing equipment or special-purpose buildings. To be eligible for the credit, firms must have paid California sales taxes or use taxes on the equipment purchases. The MIC may be claimed in addition to any enterprise zone franchise tax credits.

Research and Development Credit. California also provides firms supporting research conducted in the state a credit of 11 percent for research done in house and 24 percent for basic research payments to another entity. For fixed-price contracts, only a percentage of excess research costs would be allowable. This credit would not apply to the FACO activities because most or all research relating to FACO will be conducted during the program's SDD phase. SDD activities will take place in Texas, and therefore this tax credit is not included in our analysis.

JSF Tax Credits. In 1998, the California Assembly passed Assembly Bill 2797, which created two new tax credits—the JSF Directed Wage Credit and JSF Directed Property Tax Credit—that would allow Lockheed Martin and other California-based subcontractors that manufacture components for ultimate use in the JSF program to deduct some wage and investment costs from franchise taxes. The JSF Directed Wage Credit would provide a credit against franchise taxes for direct labor costs for each employee who is at least 90 percent directly related to manufacturing property for ultimate use in the JSF. In 2001, the first year of the program, firms could take a credit equal to the lesser of $10,000 or 50 percent of a qualified employee's annual wages. The allowable percentage declines 10 percent each year with the maximum allowable credit at $50,000 for wages in 2005. The JSF Directed Property Tax Credit would also apply toward franchise taxes. This is a credit for 10 percent of the cost of qualified property used to manufacture or assemble the JSF, including the labor and materials required to manufacture, assemble, and install the property. Qualified property includes tangible personal property used 50 percent of the time or more in activities to manufacture property for ultimate use in the JSF and the value of any capitalized labor costs that are direct costs allocable to manufacturing activities for the JSF.

Both of these credits expire January 1, 2006. Any unused credit may be carried forward until exhausted. To date, legislation has not extended these deadlines and thus these credits would not apply to FACO activities. Staff at the California Franchise Tax Board indicate that they consider it unlikely that these credits will be extended. Hence, the credits are not included in our analysis.

SUMMARY

Comparing the economic development programs across the states, it is clear that California offers the most aggressive economic development program for aerospace manufacturing. However, total tax liabilities are greater in California than in Georgia or Texas. It is RAND's assessment that these benefits would not entirely offset these higher taxes.

Chapter Seven

ENVIRONMENTAL COSTS

This chapter discusses the primary environmental costs related to FACO and estimates the expense of addressing them. We estimate the environmental costs for four sites: three Lockheed Martin sites (Fort Worth, Palmdale, and Marietta) along with the Northrop Grumman site in Palmdale.

Environmental issues have a relatively small cost effect on FACO for three reasons. First, even though aircraft manufacturing uses many toxic, highly volatile or inflammable materials and processes that can generate environmental concerns,[1] most of these materials and processes are used during parts fabrication rather than FACO, the focus of this report. Second, the four sites under consideration are already involved in aircraft production in one way or another. Thus, many of the environmental issues have already been addressed, with the required permits obtained and remediation equipment installed. FACO operations raise environmental issues only to the extent that current facilities do not address them. For example, if painting can be done in an existing facility, new emissions-control technology might not need to be installed. Furthermore, because aircraft production already goes on at these sites, intangible costs from such things as community activism are less likely.

Three types of FACO activities are significant from an environmental management perspective: aircraft painting, engine runs, and acceptance tests—all of which primarily produce air and/or noise pollution. Air emissions include volatile organic compounds (VOCs) and

_____

[1]EPA, 1998; Salomon and Sterner, 1999.

hazardous air pollutants (HAPs) during paint operations; nitrogen oxides (NOx), VOCs, and HAPs during engine test; and noise pollution during engine run and acceptance tests.

Other environmental issues must be resolved. However, they are much less significant for FACO activities than they are for fabrication and subassembly and thus impose a smaller cost burden. These issues include hazardous material handling, storage, and disposal; petroleum, oil, and lubricant handling, storage, and emergency response; explosives storage and emergency response; health and safety, including standard hearing protection and health and safety training; and wastewater treatment. As will be discussed below, however, the costs associated with these nonair environmental issues are not expected to vary significantly across sites.

Costs fall into two categories: tangible and intangible. The former refers to direct costs associated with environmental issues—e.g., installing new air-purification equipment in a paint facility to meet state or national environmental standards. Intangible costs refer to such things as responding to community activism, which can impose a real cost, for example, by delaying production. Within the tangible cost category, there are also two types of costs: recurring and nonrecurring.

We first discuss the sources of regulated emissions as they relate to JSF FACO operations. We then turn to costs, both tangible and intangible.

EMISSIONS SOURCES

Air Emissions

Final paint operations during FACO generate regulated air emissions. VOCs and HAPs, regulated under the Clean Air Act, are emitted from the sealing, painting, depainting, bonding, and finishing processes from material storage, mixing, application, drying, and cleaning. Organic solvents are used as carriers for the paint or sealant and as chemical-coating removers. In the past, aerospace paints and coatings have been solvent-based and thus have contained high concentrations of VOCs.[2] According to our conversations with the JSF Program Office and Lockheed Martin, the JSF design has two features that, if successfully utilized, will reduce VOC emissions. First, the use of appliqué coating will reduce the amount of painting required (at the time of this writing, the amount of appliqué that will be used is undetermined, but it is expected that at least some painting will occur). Second, more-extensive use of aqueous-based paints and low-VOC coatings will lead to lower emissions. A preliminary Lockheed Martin estimate of VOC emissions is 0.105 tons per aircraft, based on analogy to the F-16. (If appropriate appliqué or low-VOC paints and improved application procedures are developed before production begins, these emissions could be reduced.) Such HAPs as toluene, xylene, methyl-ethyl-ketone, and methyl-isobutyl-ketone are present as well. According to Lockheed Martin data, HAP emissions per aircraft are likely to be on the order of 50–75 percent of VOC emissions or 0.053–0.079 tons per aircraft. The other source of air emissions is running the engines, which generates NOx, hydrocarbons, particulate matter, and carbon monoxide. The JSF engine, currently in development, is a derivative of the Pratt & Whitney F119 engine, and these emissions rates are not releasable at this time. Therefore, the Lockheed Martin estimates of emissions use the F-15's

Table 7.1

Total Annual Air Emissions Estimates for a Maximum Production Rate of 17 Aircraft per Month (in tons per year)

Operation	VOCs	NOx	PM	CO	Total Hydro- carbons
Paint[a]	21.42	0.00	0.00	0.00	0.00
Engine test[b]	0.80	15.11	0.93	4.32	0.81

[a]Assuming a maximum rate of 204 aircraft per year and based on an analogy to the F-16 paint system, 60 gallons of two-part polyurethane coatings.
[b]Assuming a maximum rate of 7 uninstalled and 204 installed engines per year and the F-15 F100-PW-229 engine emissions rates.

_____

[2]EPA, 1998; Salomon and Sterner, 1999.

F100-PW-229 engine emissions rates,[3] likely test times, and power settings. Estimates of JSF air emissions by activity appear in Table 7.1.

Noise

Engine and aircraft flight tests make substantial noise, which is regulated through local ordinances and Occupational Safety and Health Administration (OSHA) regulations. Typically, local ordinances covering nuisance noise will restrict flight operations by location, duration, and time of day. OSHA standards cover allowable exposures, the use of personal protective gear, and other noise-mitigation measures.

The JSF engines will not make substantially more noise than other aircraft tested at the three sites. During the CDP, the F119 engine near-field (less than 100 ft) noise levels were comparable to legacy aircraft (F-16, F-18, AV-8B). The far-field (more than 1,000 ft) noise levels were considerably less using JSF flight profiles. These data imply that FACO activities will not significantly affect community acceptance of the JSF program in terms of noise issues.

Other Environmental Issues

Other environmental issues that crop up during FACO are wastewater treatment, hazardous materials handling, hazardous waste treatment and disposal, fuel handling, and explosives storage and handling.

Wastewater treatment will be necessary because, during surface preparation, cleaning, and coating, solvents may be rinsed into wash waters or spilled into floor drains. According to Lockheed Martin, the cleaning of paint booths will generate a nominal amount of wastewater—about 1,000 gallons per month when production is at the maximum rate of 17 aircraft per month—a fraction of the overall wastewater generated at the sites each month, which may total as much as 1 million gallons.

---

[3]The F100-PW-229 engine used on the F-15 is similar in size and thrust to the F119 engine, a derivative of which will be developed for the JSF.

Hazardous materials are normally present in sealants (although Lockheed Martin's sealants are nonhazardous), adhesives, petroleum products and synthetic lubricants and fuels, cooling and deicing fluid, and batteries. Inorganic coatings containing hazardous materials, such as chromium and cadmium, might also be used. (Lockheed Martin's current plans for the JSF include the use of chromium-free primers and no chrome or cadmium plating unless there is no other technologically equivalent material available.) In addition, various solid and liquid wastes, including waste solvents, blast media, paint chips, and spent equipment, may be generated throughout painting operations (and spot-depainting to the extent this is performed in FACO). Painting can generate solid wastes from overspray caught by emissions-control devices—e.g., paint booth filtration systems, depainting if necessary during rework (spent blast media, chips, and paint sludge), paint equipment and bay cleanup operations, and paint disposal. Used petroleum and synthetic solids and fluids are hazardous wastes and must be treated and disposed according to Resource Conservation and Recovery Act standards. Lockheed Martin states that it recycles these materials wherever possible to minimize the hazardous waste stream. Again, however, most of these materials are likely to be used during fabrication; Lockheed Martin estimates, by URF cost, that 2 percent of all hazardous materials used during manufacture will be used during FACO.[4]

FACO operations also involve safety issues related to explosives handling and storage capability for those explosives used in the ejection seat. Aircraft operations will necessitate fuel storage and spill-response capability. Most of these issues are covered under DoD regulations and safety standards and require facilities and equipment. Lockheed Martin has stated that it anticipates no significant changes will be required to address JSF FACO compared with legacy FACO operations.

In sum, all of these issues are expected to involve relatively minimal expense and management time during FACO. Most of the hazardous material handling and surface preparation or priming will occur during fabrication and minor assembly. Therefore, while the estimated

_____

[4]Discussions with Scott Fetter, Lockheed Martin, JSF ESH WBS 5460 Lead, 2001.

FACO portion of these costs is included in our analysis, a detailed analysis of the costs and potential variability across sites (also anticipated to be minimal) was not performed.

ENVIRONMENTAL COMPLIANCE COSTING APPROACH

Background

Environmental, health, and safety costs include all the recurring and nonrecurring activities associated with planning, permitting, and National Environmental Policy Act (NEPA) analysis; community reporting; employee training; hazardous material handling; wastewater treatment; disposal fees; operations safety; employee health monitoring; fire hazards; and pollution prevention that may occur during the life-cycle phase of interest (in this case, FACO).

The 1995 Defense Authorization Act, Section 815, requires environmental cost analysis to be included in the overall life-cycle cost analysis of all major defense acquisition programs. Acquisition Regulation DoD 5000.2R requires these costs be included in life-cycle estimates and also requires a programmatic environmental, safety, and health evaluation (PESHE). The PESHE describes the program managers' strategy for meeting environmental health and safety requirements, establishes responsibilities, and identifies how progress will be tracked. DoD's Cost Analysis Improvement Group (CAIG) guidance for program office estimates is that they must contain environmental costs including pollution prevention, compliance, remediation, restoration, conservation, litigation, liability, added management or overhead, operations and maintenance, and demilitarization and disposal. However, environmental costs do not need to be separated unless they are a significant cost or risk to life-cycle costs.

According to the Air Force Materiel Command's *Environmental, Safety, and Health Cost Analysis Guide,* the environmental-associated costs during acquisition are a minimal part of the total life-cycle environmental cost (EER Systems, 1998). From a total life-cycle cost point of view, the operations phase has much more significant implications (in large part because of its duration) for DoD than manufacturing activities. This is not to belittle the importance of planning and assessing environmental issues during acquisition. Careful planning and analysis is necessary for smooth and timely operations and to ensure that no costly delays occur. In a 1995 DSMC survey of 118 weapon system programs, 70 percent of the programs responded that environmental issues had an impact on their program, and 63 percent stated that their programs were affected in two or more ways. Most of the effects were detrimental: Reports cited increased cost (76 mentions), followed by schedule delays (38), degraded system performance (10), and inability to meet system requirements (6) as the most common (Noble, 1995, Table 12-3, unnumbered pages).

Despite these effects, detailed information on the environmental portion of weapon systems costs is not generally available. Particularly during acquisition, these costs are most often included in overhead and are not easily disentangled. Moreover, historically these costs have not been identified on the cost analysis requirements document. One Aerospace Industries Association estimate suggests that between 8 percent and 30 percent of a weapon systems' *overall life-cycle cost* (which encompasses much more than production) stems from environmental, health, and safety issues.[5] Lockheed Martin estimates that environmental costs associated with JSF FACO are a small fraction of overall acquisition costs.

Environment Cost Estimating Overview

We have tailored our analysis to focus on the major environmental issue during FACO, which is air emissions. There are differences across the potential FACO sites. The Fort Worth and Marietta sites are in "serious" nonattainment areas for ozone.[6] Thus, similar control technologies and other measures to reduce VOC emissions (contributors to ground-level ozone) will be required at both sites. Palmdale is in a "severe" nonattainment area for ozone. Thus, this site will have stricter standards placed on VOC emissions and other measures. Fort Worth and Marietta are in attainment for the other criteria pollutants; Palmdale is out of compliance with California

---

[5]AIA, 1997. For some weapon system types, such as chemical weapons, the demilitarization and disposal expenses of the life cycle can be quite large.

[6]"Nonattainment" areas are those regions that do not meet the primary standard for criteria pollutants established by the EPA. There are five classifications of nonattainment for ground-level ozone: marginal, moderate, serious, severe, and extreme.

standards for particulate matter. (See Appendix D for discussions on environmental regulations and air-quality standards.)

Other possible causes for cost variation, such as community activism and enforcement activities, may influence cost directly or indirectly through schedule risk and operations flexibility. These are discussed in detail later in this chapter.[7]

Aggregate-level analyses of plant-siting decisions, as well as interviews with national associations and several large corporations, suggest that environmental regulatory stringency is a minor factor in plant location decisions.[8]

No quantitative information is available on state-to-state differences in compliance costs, regulatory stringency, or complete permitting times and expenses.[9] The indexes commonly used, such as League of Conservation Voters State Scorecard and the Free Index, do not focus on cost differences and mostly represent a subjective judgment of political climate, environmental quality indicators, and regulatory standards.[10]

---

[7]The trend in the private sector and in DoD is to treat environmental, safety, and occupational health issues together. While the compliance costs for health and safety issues are included in our cost estimates, their likely effect on FACO location decisions did not warrant detailed analysis.

[8]Oates, 1998; Gray, 1997. We also gathered data from personal contacts with several large corporations, 2001; Ellen Davis of the National Association of Manufacturers, 2001; and Chuck MacCary of DEALTEK, 2001. Interviews with personnel in state government and in DoD support this conclusion as well.

[9]Permitting fees and statutory time lines are provided by some states. However, there is no information on the true costs (those that include administrative expenses borne by the company) and preparatory times. For some years, the Department of Commerce conducted an annual survey of pollution abatement and control expenditures (PACE data). This survey was suspended in 1994. One analysis of data, which controlled for state industrial composition, gave counterintuitive results (Levinson, 1999). A subsequent conversation with Dr. Levinson indicated these indexes were too aggregate a measure to use for our analysis. We also were concerned that the full effects of the Clean Air Act Amendments (CAAA) were not represented in the data.

[10]Several indexes have been cited in the literature. These include: *Conservation Fund Index*, which evaluates information on land-use characteristics, environmental characteristics, League of Conservation Voters' assessment of congressional delegation voting records, existence of state Environmental Impact Statement processes, and statutory language related to land use; *Free Index*, which is a onetime index (1991) of 256 measures of public policy and environmental quality; and the *League of Conservation Voters*, which performs annual scoring of environmental interest in

Our research also suggests that less variability in environmental stringency can be found across states compared with that of the 1980s, particularly because federal laws have leveled the playing field.[11] However, there are differences in the type of control technology required in different areas. There is also some evidence that nonattainment areas have less growth in polluting industries, and that states with tougher standards (as determined by political climate and regulatory stringency measures, not directly by cost) have fewer new plants.[12] In addition, interviewees expressed opinions regarding the difficulties in working with various states based on anecdotal information. Finally, the historical trend in environmental regulation has been toward more-stringent control. While we expect this trend to continue, it is not possible to predict its effect on required pollution-control technology and associated costs.

Our analysis relies heavily on information provided by Lockheed Martin and Northrop Grumman, validated when possible by independent sources. As mentioned earlier, environmental costs for acquisition are typically included in overhead accounts. Therefore, disentangling these costs, particularly for a subset of production, is difficult. Furthermore, there is a dearth of independent information readily available, and collecting such data, if possible, would be time-intensive and well beyond the scope of this study.[13]

The costs associated with each alternative location were determined by calculating the nonrecurring investment required to meet environmental standards for anticipated FACO operations at the site combined with the recurring estimated environmental costs arising from FACO operations. Because air emissions during painting, coating, rework, and engine run are the most significant environmental emissions during FACO, these costs are identified separately. Because the final sites selected for detailed analyses are existing aircraft-manufacturing facilities, uncertainty regarding community

---

states based on assessment of senators' and representatives' voting records on national legislation.

[11]Levinson, 1999; Gray, 1997; Oates, 1998.

[12]Gray, 1997.

[13]Based on our review of the literature and available briefings, contacts with major corporations, and interviews with staff members in PA&E/CAIG, OUSD/ES, JSF Program Office, NAVAIR, ANG/CEV.

relations (about noise, traffic, etc.) and potential schedule delays as a result of permitting are less than they would be if the facilities were built from scratch (in greenfields, for example). Assuming the facilities remain in good standing—and all indications are that they will— each will likely have most of the necessary management systems, basic permits, and equipment in place, mitigating cost variability and uncertainty.

COMPLIANCE COSTS FOR AIR EMISSIONS

The facilities and equipment requirements to control air emissions are presented in Table 7.2. Table 7.3 contains estimates of the costs of the environmental technologies. Table 7.4 summarizes the air emissions and control costs at each of the four sites. Information on the special air environmental control technology and equipment is treated here; facility investment requirements are addressed in Chapter Three.

As each of the tables indicates, while standard environmental costs are associated with each facility, FACO activities will trigger regulations or costs unique to the location of the facility, based on state and local environmental regulations. Because each of the three states uses the Clean Air Act as the basis, or "floor," for its air emissions regulations, certain regulatory similarities exist in terms of threshold values that each facility must comply with. However, permitting flexibility, emissions banking systems, additional emissions standards based on severity of nonattainment areas, and state-assessed fees all could contribute to increasing or limiting costs associated with environmental regulations during the FACO process.

The estimated emissions from the FACO process are the same across the sites. Adding up across the different sources in Table 7.2, assembling and checking out 204 aircraft a year is expected to result in 25.1 tons of VOC emissions, 15 tons of NOx emissions, and 0.9 tons of particulate-matter emissions. These estimates are based on past FACO experiences. If greater use of water-based paints occurs or if appliqué is used extensively, then VOC emissions could be lower.

Below, we discuss the findings on environmental compliance costs for each site.

Table 7.2

Facilities and Equipment Required to Control Air Emissions

Facility	Estimated Annual FACO Operations Emissions by Pollutant[a]	Environmental Control Equipment Required	Equipment Investment Cost	Equipment Annual Operations and Maintenance
Paint facility[b]	VOCs = 21 tons	All sites: three-stage Aerospace NESHAP-compliant paint filters	Three-stage filters: $1,000 per paint booth[d]	Three-stage filters: $333 filter replacement per paint booth[d]
		All sites: NESHAP-compliant high-velocity, low-pressure spray guns	$400 per gun (robotic paint facilities have two guns per paint booth; normal paint booths one gun)	$500 per gun
		Lockheed Martin–Palmdale: AVAPCD BACT will require 96%+ control device for 650,000 cubic ft per minute if new construction or extensive modification required	96%+ device: $20,000,000[e]	96%+ device: $2,000,000[e]
		Northrop Grumman–Palmdale: convert existing depaint facility to a paint facility and install new depaint equipment in another building	$10,000,000	$0
Appliqué area[c]	VOCs = 0.016 tons per aircraft = 3.300 tons			

Table 7.2—continued

Facility	Estimated Annual FACO Operations Emissions by Pollutant[a]	Environmental Control Equipment Required	Equipment Investment Cost	Equipment Annual Operations and Maintenance
Hush house	NOx = 15 tons, PM = 0.9 tons, VOCs = 0.8 tons, CO = 4.32 tons, HAPs unknown	All sites: No BACT requirement for jet engines		
Fuel barn/facility	VOCs = 0, HAPs = 0 (Enclosed fueling systems)	N/A		
Explosives Storage	N/A	N/A		
Fuel handling and spill response equipment	N/A	N/A	Rolled into general overhead costs	

[a] Assuming 204 aircraft per year.
[b] Emissions estimate assumes no appliqué and similar paint systems to the F-16. If new application technologies were used, VOC emissions would be lower.
[c] Based on experience with the F-16. If aqueous-based paints, low-VOC coatings, and appliqué are used extensively, VOC emissions could be lower.
[d] Six booths required for maximum rate of 17 aircraft per month. A reduction in the number of paint booths could occur with a production rate between 11 and 13 aircraft per month. Lockheed Martin was unsure of the exact breakpoint that would reduce the number of paint booths required.
[e] This incinerator is scaled on production rate. The given cost assumes a facility with six paint booths.

Table 7.3
Environmental Analyses and Permitting Costs

Cost Source	Lockheed Martin–Fort Worth	Lockheed Martin–Marietta	Lockheed Martin–Palmdale	Northrop Grumman–Palmdale
Air Permits				
Permit to construct and new source review (nonrecurring expenses)	$50,000 for hush house	$50,000 for paint facility $50,000 for hush house	$10,000 for paint facility $10,000 for hush house	$10,000 for hush house
Permit to operate (recurring expenses)	No additional fees required for FACO	No additional fees required for FACO	$500 per year for paint facility $200 per year for hush house $200 for appliqué area	$200 per year for hush house $200 for appliqué area
NEPA Analyses[a] (nonrecurring)	$60,000	$60,000	$160,000	$160,000
California Environmental Quality Analyses (nonrecurring)	N/A	N/A	Included in $10,000 permit	Included in $10,000 permit

[a]Expenses *may* apply if any new construction or extensive modification to existing structures is required. Expenses should be applied only once, and cover analyses for any combination of new construction.

Table 7.4

Summary of Air Emissions and Control Costs

Facility	Nonrecurring Costs[a]	Recurring Costs[b]	Emissions Banking System	Flex-Permitting
Lockheed Martin–Fort Worth	$110,000	$0	Yes—credits expire after 60 months, if banked after January 2, 2001; 120 months if prior to January 2, 2001	Yes
Lockheed Martin–Marietta	$160,000	$31 per ton over emissions thresholds	Yes—credits do not expire, but they do depreciate	No
Lockheed Martin–Palmdale	$180,000 plus $20,000,000 if new or extensively modified paint facility required[c]	$900 + $2,000,000 if new or extensively modified paint facility required[c]	Yes—credits do not expire or depreciate	No
Northrop Grumman–Palmdale	$170,000 + $10,000,000	$400	Yes—credits do not expire or depreciate	No

[a]Nonrecurring costs include equipment investment costs, NEPA analysis, and permitting costs.

[b]Recurring costs include annual equipment operations and maintenance, inspection, and annual fees.

[c]$20 million control technology and associated maintenance costs may not be required if extensive use of appliqué and water-based paints substantially reduces VOC emissions during painting. However, we cannot definitely assert that improved technology will be available by the time production starts.

Fort Worth

The primary costs at Lockheed Martin's Fort Worth site are associated with permits to construct and New Source Reviews (NSRs), and, because the plant is government-owned and contractor-operated, the requisite NEPA environmental analysis must be performed. An NSR is needed to construct a hush house, if required, while the NEPA analysis is required to address the construction of the hush house and paint facility, as well as the modification of a historical building at the facility. These nonrecurring costs total $110,000. Because the Lockheed Martin facility in Fort Worth has a Flexible Air Permit from the state of Texas, it is allowed to construct a new eight-bay paint facility under its existing air permit, provided the new facility meets the control technology standards as required by the permit. It is Lockheed Martin's assessment that an NSR will not be required for the paint facility.

Annual inspection costs to ensure compliance with air emissions regulations are $12,500 for the Fort Worth facility as a whole. However, these costs will be incurred with or without FACO. Thus, the additional inspection and maintenance costs stemming from FACO are zero.[14]

The Flexible Air Permit also allows Lockheed Martin to increase air emissions up to a facilitywide cap. Lockheed Martin can emit up to 372 tons of VOCs per year without any additional controls being installed. This contrasts with Palmdale, where Best Available Control Technology (BACT) will need to be installed on a new or extensively modified paint facility even though emissions remain below the facility cap.

Marietta

Nonrecurring costs in Marietta are similar to those Lockheed Martin would require at Fort Worth, because both sites are government-

---

[14]According to Lockheed Martin, December 20, 2001.

owned and contractor-operated and fall under NEPA requirements.[15] However, because Georgia does not offer Air Flexibility Permits, Lockheed Martin assumes an additional $50,000 for NSR of the paint facility. Georgia's annual fees associated with the Title V permit are considerably lower than those in Texas. Lockheed Martin has worked with the state of Georgia extensively to streamline its permitting process, with one permit covering the entire facility. The fees must be paid with or without FACO, however, so no incremental operating permit costs arises from FACO.

As is the case with Fort Worth, Marietta is in a serious nonattainment area and must offset increases in emissions once facilitywide emissions exceed certain levels. These thresholds are 100 tons per year for VOCs, 50 tons per year for NOx, and 100 tons per year for particulate matter. Lockheed Martin reports that, even with JSF FACO, VOC emissions will not exceed the 100-ton threshold, thus no emissions offsets would be required. NOx emissions currently exceed the threshold, so additional emissions arising from FACO must be offset. Emissions can be offset in two ways. First, Lockheed Martin can reduce emissions from existing sources. This could be accomplished by installing new non-FACO emissions-control equipment or by reducing non-FACO production at the site. Second, Lockheed Martin emissions can be offset by buying credits through Georgia's Emissions Banking Program.[16] If Lockheed Martin were unable to procure credits, it would have to pay $31 per ton of emissions over the threshold. Because Lockheed Martin plans to install new production technology—independent of FACO—that will reduce NOx emissions from other production programs at the site,[17] we do not

---

[15]According to Lockheed Martin, much of the equipment used for the F-22, such as the hush house and paint facilities, could be converted to handle the JSF. However, modifications will be extensive enough to require new source review.

[16]This emissions banking program in Georgia is modeled on the Texas emissions banking system, but, unlike in Texas, emissions credits in Georgia do not expire. Credits in Georgia are discounted after a certain period: 20 percent for VOCs and 30 percent for NOx. At the Fort Worth facility, the credits banked must be used within 60 months from the day they are awarded, if banked after January 2, 2001. Any credits awarded on or before January 2, 2001, must be used within 120 months from the time they were awarded (Texas Administrative Code, Title 30, Part 1, Chapter 101, Subchapter H, Division 1, Rule §101.302[d][2]).

[17]Lockheed Martin is planning to replace two old boilers, which will substantially reduce NOx emissions at the site.

expect Lockheed Martin will need to buy emissions credits or pay fines for FACO production.[18]

Lockheed Martin–Palmdale

The major difference between Lockheed Martin's facilities in Palmdale and its facilities in Texas and Georgia is that in Palmdale it must install BACT if a new paint facility is constructed, while at the other sites emissions credits can be used to offset the emissions that would be eliminated by BACT. BACT must also be installed if an existing paint facility is used for JSF FACO and the emissions-control equipment is extensively modified. Antelope Valley Air Quality Management District (AVAQMD) regulations require BACT for sources that emit more than 25 lbs of VOC per day (which translates into 4.6 tons per year). Emissions from the paint facility exceed this limit based on experience from past aircraft. Note, however, that if appliqué or water-based paints are used extensively, VOC emissions might not exceed the VOC cap. Absent information on how extensively water-based paints or appliqué will be used, we assume that VOC emissions will exceed the BACT requirements. Because we also do not know if pollution-control regulations will become stricter in the next few years (which may require a new paint facility, in any case), this is a reasonable approach.

Lockheed Martin reports that existing paint facilities cannot be used for FACO. It estimates that a control device that can handle 650 cubic ft per minute for a new facility will cost $20 million.[19] Lockheed

---

[18]If the Cobb County region's air quality continues to deteriorate, forcing it to become a severe nonattainment area, then the credits Lockheed Martin has banked would allow the company to continue operation without immediate increase in costs. Also, according to Lockheed Martin environmental experts and Georgia Air Protection Branch officials, Lockheed Martin should be able to use emission credits to offset and minimize any additional emission regulations arising from other future New Source Reviews required for the FACO process (discussions with Scott Fetter, Lockheed Martin, and Terry Johnson, State of Georgia Department of Natural Resources, Environmental Protection Division, Air Protection Branch).

[19]According to Lockheed Martin, options for BACT on the paint facility include thermal oxidation (incineration), activated carbon fluidized bed, ultraviolet/ozone, system, and zeolite rotary concentrator. Lockheed Martin reports capital costs range from $20–50 per cubic foot per minute of air flow. For 650,000 cubic ft per minute, this range translates into $13.0–32.5 million. Lockheed Martin's $20 million estimate is roughly the midpoint of this range.

Martin also estimates that operation and maintenance costs for this control device will amount to $2 million per year (see Table 7.2). These costs would not be incurred at Fort Worth or Marietta.

With respect to engine noise, NSR will be required for the hush house if engines are tested before installation. Once installed in the aircraft, the engines are considered mobile sources and are not subject to regulation by the AVAQMD. The U.S. Environmental Protection Agency (EPA) sets regulations on aircraft. Lockheed Martin reports that it plans to test seven engines per year in the hush house before installation. This testing will trigger NSR; we include the costs for this in our analysis.

Emissions at the Palmdale plant exceed the thresholds that trigger offset requirements for new emissions.[20] The additional emissions from the paint facility and uninstalled engines may be offset by using emissions credits banked at the facility or by buying new credits. The Lockheed Martin facilities in the Palmdale area (Plant 10 and Sites 2 and 7 on AFP 42) have an overall emissions cap of 625 lbs per day (114 tons per year) for VOC.[21] The cap does not expire or depreciate.[22] Current VOC emissions are far below the cap, and the added VOC emissions from JSF FACO will fit under the cap. According to Lockheed Martin, existing credits are also available to offset NOx emissions from uninstalled engines. If credits are not available at the site, Lockheed Martin may be able to buy credits through a market for emissions-reduction credits. Credits can be purchased from firms or brokerages in the neighboring South Coast Air Quality Management District.[23] However, the purchase of credits is associated with unpredictable risk about their availability and price.

Environmental planning and permitting covered under NEPA requires an Environmental Assessment (EA) followed by a more-

---

[20]In the AVAQMD, offsets for new emissions must be obtained for facilities emitting more than 25 tons per year of VOC, 25 tons per year of NOx, or 100 tons per day of PM10.

[21]Bret Banks, operations manager, AVAQMD, personal communication, February 2002.

[22]Alan DeSalvio, air-quality engineer, AVAQMD, personal communication, February 2002.

[23]Automated Credit Exchange in Pasadena, Calif., is an example of such a brokerage.

extensive Environmental Impact Statement (EIS) if the EA indicates significant issues. Lockheed Martin anticipates that an EA for Fort Worth and Marietta will result in a Finding of No Significant Impact from JSF production's merely replacing decreasing F-16 and F-22 production. An EA for Palmdale will be problematic because no significant legacy aircraft production offsets the new environmental emissions from JSF production. With the lack of legacy infrastructure, Lockheed Martin anticipates conducting both an EA and EIS, which it estimates will cost $160,000.

Northrop Grumman–Palmdale

At Northrop Grumman's Palmdale facility (Sites 3 and 4 on AFP 42) a building has been permitted as a paint facility and is currently used for depainting. Northrop Grumman reports that it could move the depainting to another building and use the first building for FACO painting. Using a building already permitted for painting would mean that Northrop Grumman would not need to install BACT. The company estimates that it will cost $10 million to install depainting equipment in another facility on the site and to convert the building currently used for depainting to painting.

There are two hush houses on the Northrop Grumman site that could be used for JSF FACO. If uninstalled engines are tested in them, permits must be obtained; we assume this will cost the same as reported for the Lockheed Martin–Palmdale site. Northrop Grumman may be able to test the engines at other nearby facilities, but, for the purpose of our analysis, we assume that the entire FACO process would be done on the Northrop Grumman site.

The availability of a paint facility on the Northrop Grumman site raises the question of whether Lockheed Martin–Palmdale could lease Northrop Grumman paint facilities. Doing so could cut roughly $10 million from the costs of FACO at the Lockheed Martin–Palmdale site. A number of hurdles must be overcome for Lockheed Martin to use Northrop Grumman facilities, however. Environmental liability related to air and wastewater discharges are substantial. Issues related to security around the Northrop Grumman B-2 facilities on the site would have to be addressed. Finally, there would be workers' compensation issues related to Lockheed Martin personnel working on the Northrop Grumman site that would have to be addressed. In principle, these issues could all be resolved, but resolution is not guaranteed. Resolving these issues would take time, and might generate substantial negotiation costs. In our analysis, we calculate costs assuming FACO is done entirely on the Lockheed Martin–Palmdale site or the Northrop Grumman–Palmdale site, but cost savings from sharing facilities across the two sites merit consideration.

INTANGIBLE ENVIRONMENTAL ISSUES

Several other factors may ultimately affect environmental compliance costs and schedule at the site, but the relationship to cost is neither clear nor direct. These factors include the level of community activism and acceptance, overall regulatory atmosphere (which includes innovation, complexity, industry and government cooperation, and flexibility), and enforcement aggressiveness.

Community Activism

Community activism has delayed and even terminated projects in the past. Therefore, it is important to assess how the community accepts its corporate neighbor and whether the corporation engages and informs the public about environmental concerns or projects the company is undertaking that could change the surrounding environment.

Lockheed Martin has taken an active role in all three communities and reportedly has worked hard to maintain good corporate-government relations as well as good community relations. Such an investment in community relations has paid off in support for the JSF program in each community. Data and interviews with local officials and journalists have confirmed this assessment. At all three potential locations, environmental activism directed toward the activities undertaken or the indirect consequences of these activities—e.g., increased noise, air pollution—was negligible. For example, the Air Force is rectifying contaminated groundwater in Palmdale. Despite these environmental problems and the public concern over the safety of the drinking water, there seems to be no publicly perceived linkage to the envisioned JSF FACO process and existing groundwater contamination issues. Moreover, AFP 42, which includes Northrop Grumman, has established an environmental issues board that addresses potential environmental concerns of the community. Through this board, the plant has been able to establish a good relationship with the community.   In Texas, Lockheed Martin has also maintained a solid civic relationship with the Fort Worth community.   Conversations with the chairman of the Sierra Club's Dallas–Fort Worth chapter and other activists connected with the environmental conditions of the area were all positive about Lockheed Martin's relationship with the community over the past decades.   In Marietta and the surrounding areas, jet noise associated with the Lockheed Martin aircraft manufacturing facility has not been an issue since Lockheed began manufacturing aircraft there over 50 years ago.   In fact, the only type of complaint involving noise during that time has involved Air National Guard jets flying over residential areas.

Regulatory Atmosphere

States vary in the way they regulate environmental practices beyond what is required on the federal level, as well as in the complexity of the environmental regulations.   States where sites are being considered have different regulatory atmospheres that could affect costs for the overall FACO process.   Texas and Georgia state regulations, for the most part, are consistent with federal environmental regulations, which have established a floor for environmental compliance. California has enacted environmental regulations that, in many cases, go beyond federal requirements to contend aggressively with the pollution problems the state currently faces.

The complexity of environmental regulations is a factor because the more complex an environmental regulatory program, the greater the opportunities for failure or mistakes on the part of companies trying to comply.   Theoretically, regulatory complexity could affect costs of the overall FACO process because achieving or maintaining compliance with stringent or complex state environmental regulations might lead to significant fines or temporary plant shutdown.   The number of permits required at each of the sites being considered reflects the complexity of the regulations in each state.   Lockheed Martin–Palmdale currently has 172 air permits for its site, compared with 2 at the company's site in Fort Worth and 13 at Marietta. Northrop Grumman has 45 permits in Palmdale.[24]

While California tends to have additional and more-complex regulations than either Texas or Georgia, Lockheed Martin's and Northrop Grumman's longtime presence in the Antelope Valley and understanding of these regulations should help them avoid any of the aforementioned challenges posed by a more-complex regulatory environment. In Georgia and Texas, the levels of resources invested and systems implemented by Lockheed Martin for addressing environmental issues and its good relations with state enforcement agencies mean that regulatory problems will most likely not adversely affect the company in terms of plant shutdowns or lead to significant additional costs incurred associated with violations.

Another way for a company to address challenges posed by state environmental regulations and compliance requirements is through environmental management innovations. An environmental management system (EMS) is integrated into an organization's overall management process, identifying policies, environmental goals, measurements, authority structures, and resources necessary to achieve compliance with environmental regulations, as well as attain a level of environmental performance that goes beyond minimal compliance. In some cases, the state government works with companies to help them develop EMSs. Lockheed Martin has operated a formal EMS since 1992. The system combines occupational health aspects and environmental compliance and pollution prevention. It also allows for the development of government-corporation communication channels to monitor compliance with regulations, reducing the risk of noncompliance. Lockheed Martin–Fort Worth is currently certified by an independent third-party body to ISO 14000 standards. In 1998, Lockheed Martin–Palmdale declared itself in conformance with ISO 14001 Standard and maintains a corporatewide EMS program. For both its Palmdale and Marietta sites, Lockheed Martin is in the process of seeking third-party certification to the standard. By 2004, all sites are anticipated to be certified.[25]

---

[24]Permit information is from DCMA data.

[25]Discussion with Lockheed Martin environmental personnel. Fort Worth is already third party certified. Palmdale is seeking third-party (currently self-certified); Marietta

Enforcement Aggressiveness

Statutory authority that allows state enforcement agencies to assess penalties varies from state to state and could affect the amount of the penalty and time it takes to levy—factors that could affect cost. Both Texas and Georgia have administrative order authority, which allows enforcement agencies to fine violators without pursuing legal action. California is in the midst of a regulatory reform that will provide such authority to certain enforcement areas. But currently no plan exists to give administrative order authority to one of the most significant enforcement agencies: air-quality management districts. A combination of aggressive enforcement and more legal enforcement mechanisms could lead to a more drawn-out penalty process if violations are significant. Enforcement authority could also affect frequency of inspections because enforcement authorities in states without administrative order authority are less inclined to make numerous visits if their only recourse to achieve compliance or assess fines is through the courts.[26] Based on its experience with Lockheed Martin, California has tended to follow this pattern, with more-aggressive, but less-frequent, site inspections than the Fort Worth or Marietta site. However, given Lockheed Martin's ability to comply with state and local environmental regulations, aggressive enforcement should not be an issue.

SUMMARY

From the perspective of environmental costs, the primary difference between the sites is the cost of controlling air emissions. Air pollution is worse in the Palmdale area than it is in Fort Worth or Marietta, and more-stringent air pollution control equipment is required in Palmdale. VOC emissions during the FACO painting process are the major source of concern. No existing paint facilities at the Lockheed Martin–Palmdale site can be used for FACO. The emissions-control technology required on a new paint facility would cost an estimated $20 million to install and $2 million per year to operate and main-

---

is also seeking third-party certification. Within two years, all sites will be third-party certified.

[26]GAO, 2000, p. 40.

tain. These costs need not be incurred at Fort Worth or Marietta. Existing paint facilities are available at the Northrop Grumman site, so new air pollution control equipment would not have to be installed there. However, it would cost an estimated $10 million to reconfigure existing facilities at the site to accommodate FACO painting. Lockheed Martin–Palmdale could, in principle, use Northrop Grumman paint facilities, but a number of security, environmental, and workplace safety issues would likely be difficult to resolve.

If paint technology or the use of appliqués for the JSF evolves over the next five years during SDD, currently required pollution control investments might be avoided. However, pollution standards might be tightened during the same period. We follow a conservative approach and assume that investments will be required.

There is no basis to prefer one site over another based on community and nongovernmental organization activism, previous violations, or the relations the facilities have with the community. No location has environmental costs significant enough to make a compelling case for not locating FACO there. Although the Palmdale site may be at somewhat of a disadvantage in terms of regulatory atmosphere and enforcement aggressiveness, it appears that, while adding some risk, any California-specific issues in these areas are manageable.

Chapter Eight

OTHER COST FACTORS:
STEALTH, SUPPLIERS, AND ENERGY

Many factors affect the cost of FACO, but some have less effect than others. This chapter discusses three factors that have only modest effect on the cost of FACO operations: the low-observable (or stealth) component, the supplier and technical support bases at the different locations (including transportation costs and supplier support), and energy.

JSF STEALTH

The shape of the JSF, special technologies, and special coatings give the aircraft its low-observable characteristics. In this section, we discuss issues relating to the cost of stealth for JSF FACO. Stealth technology is a sensitive and often classified subject, which limits the content of this section. This discussion relies entirely on unclassified data, including what is available in open literature and received from U.S. government sources and from Lockheed Martin. It includes data on JSF stealth requirements during manufacturing and, more specifically, during the FACO process.

An Overview of the JSF Stealth Requirements

Stealth is a very important feature of the survivability of JSF during combat. The need has been clear from the beginning of the program and is specified in the official documents laying out operational requirements for the JSF:[1]

---

[1]JSF Program Office, 1998.

The survivability of legacy aircraft against the projected threats necessitates allocating large portions of the force structure to the Suppression of Enemy Air Defenses (SEAD) role. The current threat detection systems force the aircrew into taking reactive vice proactive measures. Many current aircraft must rely on force packaging support assets for surface-to-air missile (SAM) suppression (such as EA-6B) or external carriage of [electronic attack] systems for survivability. Most current countermeasures have limited capability against advanced threats and are not compatible with [low-observable] aircraft. Analysis shows that conducting a theater campaign against a capable enemy results in high aircraft attrition and leaves significant threats operational. To be affordable and effective against advanced threats, stealth technology must be designed into the basic aircraft. Situational awareness afforded by advanced avionics will play a significant role in survivability.

In general, aircraft stealth is achieved through a complicated mix of airframe shape, special materials, and special technologies designed to reduce the ability of the opposition to detect, track, and attack the aircraft. JSF design incorporates the following features to achieve stealth:

- Radio frequency signature control to minimize susceptibility and maximize the probability of survival against projected radio frequency threats.

- Electro-optical/infrared (EO/IR) technology to minimize susceptibility and maximize the probability of survival against projected EO/IR threats.

- Covert lighting technology to minimize susceptibility to projected threats' optical and night-vision systems.

- Ability to eliminate, reduce, mask, or control electronic emissions to minimize detection, tracking, or engagement by a threat with minimal degradation to mission effectiveness.

- Ability to minimize the threat posed by acoustic tracking systems.

JSF Airframe Stealth Approach During the Manufacturing Process

The airframe stealth is achieved through two main approaches: radar-absorbing structures (RASs) and radar-absorbing material (RAM). Older stealth aircraft, such as the F-117, use time-consuming techniques that have been superseded; in those aircraft, the airframe is almost entirely covered with RAM, which made the final finishing stages of the manufacturing process very critical.[2] The F-22 fighter, a newer airframe, uses RAS on the sharp edges around the wing, tail surfaces, and body and spray-on RAM only around the edges of doors and control surfaces. Its skins are covered with conductive metallic coating, which prevents radar energy from penetrating the composite skin and a top coat to suppress the infrared signature.[3] This approach has reduced the final finishing efforts, but it still consumes a significant part of FACO labor.

The JSF airframe will employ a more innovative approach to implement this requirement, which should reduce the effort required during the FACO stage. Table 8.1 compares the legacy approach with the JSF approach. The JSF stealth approach minimizes the use of time-consuming manufacturing processes, including the application of radar absorbing sheets of coating material and finishing material that require long cure cycles. Also, use of new design tools should allow for early verification of assembly of radar absorbing structures.

The JSF subassemblies will be delivered in modules with many of the subsystems, including some special stealth technologies, already integrated. The goal is to have most of the final finishing work accomplished before FACO. During the manufacturing process of these modules, paints, coatings, and sealants will have already been applied at the detail part or subassembly stations. In many cases, before the FACO stage, surfaces will be cleaned and prepared, the fasteners will be filled and faired, and the surfaces will be sprayed,

---

[2]Sweetman and Cook, 2001.

[3]Sweetman and Cook, 2001.

Table 8.1

**Comparison of the Stealth Implementation in the
Legacy System to the JSF Approach**

	Legacy Systems	JSF Approach
Treatment	RAM—Sheet, Manual Spray (F-117)	No sheet material, minimal use, advanced robotic spray
	Tape—most panels/doors require high degree of alignment (B-2 and F-117)	Minimal use of tape, less labor intensive process, robotic application
	Butter—most panels (B-2, F-117, F-22)	Minimize, short cure material-form in-place gaskets
	Experimental products and significant producibility issue (F-117 and B-2)	Use of CAD/CAM tools allows for early verification of the manufacturing processes
	Numerous types of materials (B-2 more than 450)	Few types (less than 30)
Structure	High tolerances	Modern manufacturing process can maintain high level of tolerances
	Complex integration	Simplified integration
Apertures	Small number of sensors (F-117)	EO/IR and use of numerous apertures

coated, and sealed. Lockheed Martin estimates that about 70 percent of the work related to stealth will be done before FACO.[4]

During the final finishing step of FACO, the aircraft will need to be coated with RAM. (For example, Lockheed Martin is attempting to develop an appliqué material to be used as the final topcoat.) This effort accounts for about 28 percent of FACO operations standard hours.[5] Significant attention to the fidelity of the aircraft mold line is required, and it will be verified using a turntable mechanism. Finally, the JSF airframe will be tested in an anechoic chamber where its radar cross section (RCS) will be tested and recorded.

---

[4]Lockheed Martin's response to RAND questionnaire, February 2002.

[5]Lockheed Martin briefing to RAND, May 7–8, 2001.

Costs of Stealth for JSF FACO

In addition to the labor required for stealth implementation during the FACO process, JSF FACO stealth processes have four main tooling and facility requirements or cost drivers. A secure facility or secure space on the factory floor of about 200×200 ft with special radar absorbing features will be needed. A certain number of tools will be needed for the coating, including robotic coating devices, appliqué equipment, and surface finish test equipment. A low-observable verification turntable device, required to test the aircraft RCS, needs to be in a secure and air-conditioned facility. A ground test radar will be required to collect RCS signature information, which will then be analyzed by dedicated computers and other analytical tools. Some number of workers with clearances will be needed to do the work. The facilities, tools, and equipment required to ensure and verify stealth will be needed at all sites and have been included in the cost analysis.

Because of the innovative nature of the stealth, with much of the work being done during the fabrication and subassembly stage, Lockheed Martin estimates that not all FACO workers will need clearances, perhaps only 20 percent. Given the number of workers holding clearances at each site, we estimate that cleared workers can be transferred from other programs that will be finishing as JSF production ramps up. Alternatively, new employees can be hired into jobs that do not require clearances for ongoing programs, and cleared workers can be transferred to the JSF work. Hence, no site has a significant determinable advantage over any other site, and the costs for worker clearances are not included in the model. In any case, Lockheed Martin estimates that the costs to get clearances are relatively modest, perhaps $1,000 per worker. The bigger issue with clearances is the time required for the government to complete background investigations. However, given that JSF production activities will be relatively predictable and the time to get a clearance is known (about 12–18 months), this issue can be managed with appropriate advanced planning.

THE SUPPLIER AND TECHNICAL SUPPORT BASE, SUPPLIERS, AND TRANSPORTATION COSTS

We turn next to the issue of the supplier base. The congressional language mandating this study calls for consideration of supplier and technical support bases. We address that issue in this section. We also discuss the costs of two other issues relating to suppliers. The first is supplier support of the FACO process through on-site supplier representation. The second is the possible impact of the relative costs of transporting FACO inputs to the different potential FACO sites. Neither of these issues has proven to be a significant driver of FACO costs.

Supplier and Technical Support Base

One of the concerns expressed in the legislation mandating the study is to ensure that the choice of the ultimate FACO location takes into account local "supplier and technical support bases." Lockheed Martin has stated that the location and use of FACO suppliers will remain independent of domestic FACO location.

The various processes of FACO were described in Chapter One. Purchased items integrated during the FACO process are relatively high-tech and complex, including certain avionics and the landing gear. Suppliers of these items sell to a national, rather than a local, market. Lockheed Martin has already selected the suppliers for the FACO inputs, and these companies already have existing production locations. While one potential FACO site or another might have a robust supplier and technical support base, this type of support is more important for the fabrication stage, which depends more on outsourcing to such local contractors as machine shops. Hence, RAND has determined that the existence of a robust local supply and technical support base is not an issue for JSF FACO. For reference, a list of FACO suppliers and their production locations appear in Table 8.2.

Table 8.2

FACO Suppliers

	Location	Providing	Tier
Lockheed Martin Aero	Palmdale, Calif.	Edges	IWTA
Northrop Grumman	Palmdale, Calif.	Center fuselage	Prin. sub
TRW Radio Systems	San Diego, Calif.	Communication, navigation, identification	1st
Parker Aerospace	Irvine, Calif.	Flight controls	2nd
Lockheed Martin Aero	Fort Worth, Texas	Forward fuselage, wings, weapons bay doors	Prime
Hamilton Sundstrand	Rockford, Ill.	Electrical power system	1st
Smiths Industries	Grand Rapids, Mich.	Fuselage remote interface unit and tactical data equipment	1st
General Electric	Evendale, Ohio	Engine (2nd source)	GFE
Goodrich Corporation	Cleveland, Ohio; Fort Worth, Texas	Landing gear system	1st
TBD	TBD	Nose wheel steering	2nd
Honeywell/Dunlop	South Bend, Ind./United Kingdom	Wheels	2nd
Crane Hydro Air	Burbank, Calif.	Brake control system	2nd
TBD	TBD	Tires	2nd
BAE Systems Controls	Johnson City, N.Y.	Active inceptors	1st
Moog	East Aurora, N.Y.	Actuators	1st
Litton Amecom	College Park, Md.	Electronic warfare/countermeasures	2nd
Northrop Grumman Electronic	Baltimore, Md.	Radar and electro-optical sensors and systems sector	1st
Smiths Industries	Whippany, N.J.	Electrical power system	2nd
Pratt & Whitney	Hartford, Conn.	Engine	1st
BAE Systems	Nashua, N.H.	Electronic warfare/countermeasures	1st
LM Missiles and Fire Control	Orlando, Fla.	Electro-optics	2nd
BAE Systems	United Kingdom	Rear fuselage, tails	Prin. sub

Table 8.2—continued

	Location	Providing	Tier
Fokker–Aerostructure	The Netherlands	Doors	1st
Fokker–Elmo	The Netherlands	Wire harness	1st
Honeywell	Torrance, Calif.	Power thermal management system (PTMS)	1st
	Phoenix, Ariz.	Turbomachine assembly	2nd
	Tempe, Ariz.	Valves	2nd
	Toronto, Ontario	PTMS controller, software and sensors	2nd
	Tucson, Ariz.	Cabin pressure valves	2nd
Moog	Torrance, Calif.	Actuators	1st
Raytheon Systems	Plano, Texas	Integrated core processor	2nd
Harris Corporation	Melbourne, Fla.	Common components	2nd
EDO	North Amityville, N.Y.	Suspension and release	2nd
Rolls-Royce Allison	Indianapolis, Ind.	Lift fan	2nd
BF Goodrich	Cleveland, Ohio	Landing gear	2nd
TRW Lucas Aerospace	United Kingdom	Weapons bay door drive/drive shaft	GFE/2nd
Martin Baker	United Kingdom	Ejection seat	2nd
Rolls-Royce	United Kingdom	Lift fan/roll posts	2nd
Smiths Industries	United Kingdom	Electrical power distribution	1st
Vision Systems, International	San Jose, Calif.	Displays	1st
Kaiser Electronics, Rockwell	San Jose, Calif.	Displays	1st
Lockheed Martin Tactical Systems	Eagan, Minn.	Integrated core processor	1st
Honeywell Normair-Garrett Ltd.	United Kingdom	Life support	2nd
Boeing	Mesa, Ariz.	Gun	1st
Marion Composites	Marion, Va.	Radome	1st

SOURCE: Lockheed Martin.

Supplier Representation on Site

One of the lessons learned from previous RAND research[6] is the importance of integrating the expertise of suppliers early in the design process and throughout production. Best practice and lean manufacturing strategies that emphasize partnering with suppliers can reduce a variety of costs, including inventory holding costs, labor and space costs associated with inventories, and even costs of re-work.[7] To achieve these savings, however, coordination with suppliers takes on even more importance. Point-of-use delivery offers a good example of critical coordination activities. Point-of-use delivery involves the supplier taking responsibility for delivering the part or component directly to the location in the factory where it will be incorporated into the final product. Often, supplier representatives are on site to help manage integration of their inputs into the final product.

Lockheed Martin expects that both Pratt & Whitney and General Electric Aircraft Engines will want to have supplier representatives at the FACO site. This will not vary by choice of FACO location. However, choosing multiple FACO locations will mean that the associated costs of supplier representatives will increase proportionately. RAND estimates that five supplier representatives will be required on hand at each FACO site—this cost is included in the cost model. Our assumption is that the two engine suppliers will each have two representatives. The last individual represents "as needed" support from other suppliers.

Logistics and Transportation Costs

FACO will bring components and subassemblies from a variety of locations together at one place. One set of costs that needs to be considered when evaluating FACO location alternatives is that associated with moving these components and subassemblies to the final FACO site and storing them there.

---

[6]Cook and Graser, 2001.

[7]Cook and Graser, 2001.

Lockheed Martin plans to receive modules and components shipped from a number of different sources throughout the Unites States and Europe. For example, Northrop Grumman will assemble the center fuselage in California. Lockheed Martin will make the edges in Palmdale. The forward fuselage, wing, and weapons bay doors will be produced by Lockheed Martin in Fort Worth. Engines will come from Hartford, Conn., and radar from Baltimore, Md. Other components will come from overseas. The aft fuselage and tails will come from Salmesbury, England, and some doors will come from the Netherlands.

The choice of FACO locations will affect shipping costs. If Fort Worth is the FACO site, the forward fuselage and wing need not be shipped, just moved across the factory floor. If the FACO work is done in Palmdale, these components must be shipped to California, but the costs to ship the center fuselage and edges will largely disappear. In Marietta, where no additional work is being done, the shipping costs will have to include transporting all these components.

Lockheed has several options for shipping components to the FACO location(s). Components from domestic suppliers will be trucked. Components coming from overseas will be shipped to a common port, most likely Houston, and then trucked to their final destination. Air transport is too costly to be anything more than an emergency backup alternative. (Rail shipment offers another alternative for transport, provided the FACO location had rail access, but Lockheed said it plans to use truck shipments.)

Component size and weight are the two main drivers of shipping cost. Crate returns are an additional factor to consider because Lockheed must bear the cost of returning shipping crates to their point of origin for further use. (Some shipping containers may even need to be custom-made.) Because Lockheed Martin only provided estimates of shipping costs for their Fort Worth location, RAND used publicly available data to construct a shipping cost model.[8] This model can simulate transport costs for a variety of alternate FACO plans. Generally, the change in shipping costs arising from changing FACO locations is small—a few thousand dollars per plane if FACO

---

[8]More detail on the development of the model used to predict shipping costs can be found in Chapter Nine.

were relocated entirely to Palmdale or Marietta, less than that if only part of FACO is relocated. On an annual basis the amount is less than $1 million per year at peak production.

The other part of FACO logistics to consider is inventory cost—the cost associated with holding inventory. Inventory costs are typically taken to include interest costs (opportunity costs), depreciation, obsolescence, taxes, storage costs, handling costs, shrinkage costs, and insurance.[9] Many of these costs are subsumed into overhead costs, while others are explicitly disallowed, as will be discussed below. In any case, inventory costs would only need to be considered in the case of multiple FACO sites if it is assumed that a certain number of items are held in inventory as a buffer before integration during FACO. Current best practice minimizes these costly buffers. Furthermore, because the supplied items being incorporated during FACO are high-cost items, Lockheed Martin plans to integrate them quickly rather than hold extras.

For the minimal inventories that are held, inventory interest costs and inventory item depreciation costs are not allowable according to Federal Acquisition Regulation 31.205.

Obsolescence per se is not an issue here as a cost so much as it is a potential risk, but, at the planned rates of production, any differences in risk according to FACO strategy would be quite small. Shrinkage and insurance costs are allowable but are included in overhead rates and are captured in the overhead portion of the cost model. Lockheed Martin estimates that roughly 20,000 sq ft of storage space is needed for FACO at each location, so the use of multiple sites will entail the costs of duplicating this space. These costs are incorporated into the facilities portion of the cost model. Handling costs are an aspect of labor costs, treated as material management and material inventory control labor.

Summary of Supplier Issues

Issues involving the supplier and technical support base and transportation costs would not be materially altered by the choice of

---

[9]Tersine, 1988.

FACO strategy, whether at single or multiple locations. The cost of on-site supplier personnel costs would increase if FACO work were split among multiple locations.

ENERGY

Two of the energy factors to consider in the JSF FACO location decision are its cost and reliability. Ultimately, neither should have much effect on the location decision because the difference in the total cost of energy between sites is not great, and reliability issues are impossible to predict over the long term. This section first describes the demand for energy and then discusses the cost and reliability of electricity at the different locations.

Electricity is vital to a number of aspects of FACO. In FACO, electricity is primarily used for environmental controls, such as lighting, humidity, and temperature control. Humidity and temperature control are necessary for the precision fit of the aircraft's components. Fluctuations in heat and moisture may adversely affect the shape and tolerances of the subassembly connections. Electricity is also required for computers and to power some of the tools used in the FACO process. The coatings process and fuel activities also use electricity.

Both the cost and reliability of electricity depend on location. Table 8.3 shows the source of electric power generation for the three states with FACO facilities under consideration. Almost two-thirds of the electricity in Georgia is generated by coal, with nuclear power accounting for most of the rest. Texas receives about half of its electric power from gas and most of the rest from coal. Nuclear power accounts for about 10 percent of the total. California also uses gas for about half of its electricity, but hydroelectric and nuclear power account for about 20 percent each, with coal supplying about 1 percent of the total.

The Georgia Power Company, which serves most of the state, provides power to Marietta. The local utility in Fort Worth is the Texas Utilities Electric Company. However, Texas Electric Choice went into effect on January 1, 2002, providing the choice of electricity retail provider to both residential and nonresidential customers. The Fort

Table 8.3

Electric Power Industry Generation by Energy Source, 1999

Energy Source	California (%)	Georgia (%)	Texas (%)
Coal	1.2	64.2	39.2
Natural gas	47.2	2.7	49.2
Nuclear power	17.4	26.7	10.2
Hydroelectric power	21.1	2.3	0.3
Other	13.0	4.1	1.1

SOURCE: U.S. Department of Energy, 2001a.

Worth plant could choose a new provider before full-rate FACO operations begin. Similarly, Southern California Edison locally supplies the Palmdale area with power, but customers are free to choose another provider.

The Cost of Electricity

Little additional capital cost is required to meet FACO energy needs. FACO will require 270-volt direct current (DC) electricity, which is not normally supplied by electric utilities. Each power transformer is estimated to require an outlay of $25,000. About four would be needed at the peak JSF production rate of about 200 aircraft per year.

The bulk of energy costs will come directly from usage. These electricity costs depend on two factors: the price of electricity and electricity consumption. Specific long-term forecasts of electricity prices for industrial consumers for the utilities that supply each of these facilities do not exist.[10] The U.S. Department of Energy, through its Energy Information Administration (EIA), forecasts future energy prices at a more aggregate level. New forecasts are produced annually and published in the *Annual Energy Outlook* (AEO). The AEO for 2002 produces projections of energy outputs to 2020 (U.S. Department of Energy, 2001b). (Because of the lack of a forecast for the

---

[10]The state of California does have a forecast of electric rates for the utility that supplies Palmdale (Southern California Edison), but it only extends to 2012. The change in rates over time in this forecast is similar to the one presented below. See California Energy Commission, 2002.

period following 2020, for these calculations we presume that rates remain constant in real terms.) The heart of the AEO is the National Energy Modeling System (NEMS). NEMS uses a comprehensive series of supply-and-demand-based modules integrated to capture the market dynamics for a variety of energy sources, including oil, coal, and natural gas, and for a wide range of consumption purposes. These modules are run first at regional levels and then aggregated into a national estimate. NEMS is regularly used to provide analyses to Congress as well as to the Department of Energy. AEO 2002 focuses on the effect of long-term events on energy demand and energy prices. Events include changes in the prices and supplies of fossil fuels, developments in electricity markets, likely improvements in technology, and the impact of economic growth. AEO 2002 reflects data available as of July 2001, which included most data from 2000 but only partial data from 2001. However, AEO 2002 projections take into account the long-term contracts entered into by California to guarantee electricity supplies to the state. (If recent attempts by the state to reduce the amounts paid under those contracts prove successful, electricity costs would likely be lower at Palmdale than those presented here.)

Consumers of electricity are typically broken down into three types: residential, commercial, and industrial. Industrial users generally receive the lowest rates because they buy relatively large amounts of power and often locate closer to generation facilities. Sufficiently large users, under permissive regulatory environments, may be able to directly negotiate long-term rates with utilities for large amounts of power. (Residential users are at the other end of the rate spectrum.)

AEO 2002 forecasts regional electricity prices for industrial users of electricity. We derive from these forecasts the future percentage changes in the price of electricity paid by the facilities under consideration. The survey of facilities conducted by DCMA provides information on the average electricity rate paid for each of the locations. The percentage cost changes for the appropriate region of the country are then applied to the electricity costs reported by the locations, yielding estimates of the future rates.

Long-run electricity prices are forecast to fall somewhat in California, to fall slightly in Georgia, and to increase slightly in Texas, although much of the change is expected to take place before 2006. Despite these movements, electricity prices at the Fort Worth and Marietta facilities are still much lower than prices at either facility in Palmdale. Rates in Palmdale are roughly double those at the locations outside California.

The second component of FACO energy cost is electricity consumption. For FACO, electricity consumption is primarily driven by power and HVAC for the space needed for final assembly, painting, fueling, and low-observable testing, and by power for the run stations[11] The more planes undergoing FACO at one time, the more space is needed. However, the number of aircraft actually being assembled in that space does not significantly affect energy use. Lockheed Martin officials estimate 31.2 kWh per square foot of FACO space per year will be consumed, and 225,000 kWh per run station.[12] With Lockheed Martin's estimates of its space needs for facilities performing FACO at different rates, we can calculate the cost of electricity at the different locations and with different rates of FACO. These calculations are included in our cost analysis.

Because electricity costs are relatively low and energy's share of FACO costs is small, these electricity cost differences will have very little effect on overall FACO costs. Annual differences between the least-expensive and most-expensive energy alternatives (Marietta and Lockheed Martin–Palmdale, respectively) total in the hundreds of thousands of dollars per year. On a per-plane basis, the difference between locations is usually a few thousand dollars for any given rate of FACO.

These forecasts, put simply, are forecasts; AEO 2002 rightly notes that these forecasts are subject to many uncertainties. Future developments in technologies, significant discoveries of natural resources, changing demographic patterns, or a variety of political factors could all significantly influence these rates, especially when looking across 20 years. Strikes or severe weather could significantly affect rates for a particular area in any given year.

---

[11]Run stations are specialized locations equipped to allow testing of a plane's engine.

[12]This estimate compares favorably to results from the DCMA survey of the four facilities.

Reliability

Uncertainty about the future also applies to an energy concern still fresh in many minds: the reliability of electricity supply. FACO operations need a reliable source of electricity. Power outages mean work stoppages until lights and HVAC systems can be brought back on line. Coating operations could require significant rework if an outage occurs during the application of final finishes.

Four factors affect the reliability of electricity supply: the robustness of the fuel supply, the margin of safety (the reserve margin), transmission and distribution system capacity and weak links, and weather and storms.

As mentioned above, California's electricity supply comes from a variety of sources. Natural gas is the most common, but the state utilizes hydroelectric, coal, and nuclear power as well. Georgia is somewhat coal-dependent, and Texas uses significant amounts of both coal and natural gas. Over the next decade, natural gas is likely to play an even larger role in electricity supply in California and other states, but realistically we cannot forecast the stability of natural gas supplies 10 and 20 years hence. EIA, the Gas Research Institute, and the economic consulting firm DRI-WEFA all forecast natural gas prices to be lower (in real terms) in 2015 and 2020 than they are today (U.S. Department of Energy, 2001b). Similarly, coal price forecasts show no real appreciation in cost, and, in some instances, they show decreases for the same time horizon. None of the forecasts include any predictable future supply problems.

The reserve margin also affects reliability. If the reserve margin gets too low, it makes it difficult for the system to handle peaks in demand. In 2001, California exemplified this as demand outstripped supply. A California Energy Commission report (2002) outlines a variety of actions the state took to spur additional electricity generation and to encourage conservation to help avoid electricity outages during summer 2001 after the problems earlier in the year. To expand generation, the state worked to boost output at existing plants, to restart plants that had been recently retired, and to accelerate reviews for plants under consideration. New peak generating capacity brought on line in 2001 added roughly 5 percent to existing capacity. Conservation programs and financial incentives also proved successful in reducing electricity demand by 5–10 percent (depending on the month). As a result, the California Energy Commission finds that supplies are most likely to be sufficient to increase reserve margins and maintain reliability to 2005 and beyond.

Third, transmission and distribution system capacity and weak links are an ongoing concern. Shortages of transmission capacity can pose a problem, although they tend to occur at the same time as reserve margin difficulties. Excess power exists somewhere even during outages induced by low reserves, but the transmission lines necessary to get electricity to where it is needed may be congested.

Weather and storms are the fourth major reliability influence. Extreme heat or cold will significantly affect demand for electricity, which may cause reliability problems when coupled with low reserve margins. Storms have the potential to disrupt the transmission and distribution system by taking out power lines. For the past three years, EIA has kept track of major disturbances to power systems around the country (U.S. Department of Energy, 2001c). The EIA data on major disturbances show that none of the potential locations was affected for weather-related reasons in the past three years.

California experienced a significant problem with power reliability in 2001 because of low reserve margins, but this problem was remedied in a relatively short time. An analysis of EIA data shows that Southern California Edison experienced three major disturbances that resulted in widespread service disruption to Southern California between March and May 2001.[13] However, California went from a situation of daily potential for outages to no shortages in less than a year. Perhaps more important, in a survey conducted on RAND's behalf by DCMA, none of the facilities under consideration reported any power outages in the past five years that resulted in a work stoppage, despite the widely publicized difficulties that affected areas of California.

---

[13]The California Independent System Operator itself had six major disturbances between January 2001 and May 2001. Single disturbances occurred in California in 1999 and 2000. While Texas experienced three major disturbances in 2001, four in 2000, and three in 1999, none affected the Fort Worth area (many of them were weather-related). Georgia escaped serious disturbances in all three years for which data were available.

The time horizon between now and the start of FACO is distant. The study produced by the staff of the California Energy Commission attempts to quantify some aspects of the risk of unreliable electricity, but its predictions only extend to next year.[14] Even if a problem with reliability were to suddenly emerge next summer, between now and 2010 any part of the country would have the time and ability to fix any problems that might surface with the reliability of electricity. A gas turbine system can be fully operational in three years. Siting and permitting issues can be expedited for plants already in the planning stages. Recently retired plants can be returned to service even more quickly than new facilities can be put into place. And conservation programs and incentives can significantly reduce energy use in a matter of weeks to months.

It is not possible to say that electricity in Palmdale will be less reliable than it will be anywhere else in the country 10 years from now. With no disruptions experienced in the past five years at any of these sites, and with the difficulty of foreseeing very-low-probability events many years into the future, we cannot say with any confidence that electricity supplies will be more or less reliable at any of these locations.

---

[14]California Energy Commission, 2002. In a Monte Carlo experiment of 300 runs, the electricity supply capacity for Southern California fell below a minimum 7-percent reserve margin at peak demand in 1.3 percent of the cases for summer 2003.

MODELING THE COST IMPLICATIONS OF ALTERNATIVE FACO STRATEGIES FOR JSF PRODUCTION

Analyzing the costs of any production task can be complex. In this case, the many scenarios that must be considered make the analysis even more difficult. To analyze different work splits, we have developed a cost model that can be used to examine the effects of the cost drivers under different scenarios. We have also identified and examined a number of other issues beyond those in the congressional language to complete a full and objective evaluation of the different scenarios.

Many factors, including labor efficiency, taxes, facilities requirements, environmental constraints, would affect the cost of having additional or alternative FACO sites for JSF production. It is difficult to predict the influence of all these cost effects. Some factors could increase the total production cost of using a second site—most notably, the need for redundant facilities, tooling, and equipment. Other factors may even *decrease* the total FACO cost for a multiple-site strategy compared with a single-site one. One such factor is the incentives to hire workers. These incentives may reduce the production cost at a second site. If the number of employees that could take advantage of these incentives were limited, it might make sense to move that portion of the work that would take advantage of the incentives to that second site. How these factors combine to result in a higher or lower FACO production cost is not obvious. We have no way of knowing whether a particular FACO strategy is more or less expensive without accounting for all the relevant factors in a consistent manner.

Cost influences may not be independent of one another, which complicates the accounting. Some influences on the FACO cost affect other factors. For example, environmental regulations may require additional facilities investments, such as a thermal oxidizer to reduce emissions of VOCs. These will in turn increase power usage, and thus overhead cost, at the site. Reflecting these linkages between factors is critical to an accurate determination of cost effects. The cost model that RAND has developed enables the quantitative assessment of the cost implications of different FACO strategies. In this chapter, we describe this model and the calculations made within it.

COST ELEMENTS IN THE MODEL

The RAND model was developed in Microsoft Excel and consists of nine different modules that correspond to discrete elements of cost. These elements, which are the major cost drivers for FACO activities, are production labor, indirect costs (overhead and G&A), investments (facilities, equipment, and tooling), taxes and credits, environmental and permitting costs, transportation, power, prime and supplier management support, and fee. Generally, each module calculates the appropriate cost for each fiscal year[1] of production. Some costs, such as labor, are incurred over the entire production run (called recurring costs), while others, such as tooling and equipment, might be onetime costs or periodic (called nonrecurring costs). In this section, we describe the methodology and assumptions used to evaluate each cost element.

Production Labor

Labor is one of the largest cost components for FACO. The labor associated with FACO activities consists of two distinct types: "touch" and "support." *Touch labor* is the direct work in the production of the aircraft, including such activities as structural mate, testing, and flight operations. *Support labor* is direct labor that facili-

---

[1]For the FACO activity of the JSF program, we assume that actual costs are incurred two years after the government fiscal year in which the funds are appropriated (the gap between order and delivery).

tates FACO touch work, including engineering, quality, material inventory, and the like.   For all these elements, we used the work breakdown structure (WBS) employed by Lockheed Martin for FACO activities and modeled each as a separate component of the overall production labor.   The WBS is as follows:

- Direct Labor
  - —Fuselage structural mate
  - —Subsystem mate
  - —Final assembly and test
  - —Flight operations
  - —Manloads/incomplete task logs[2]
  - —Final finishes
- Support Labor
  - —Manufacturing engineering
  - —Tool engineering
  - —Tool manufacturing
  - —Quality
  - —Engineering
  - —Material inventory

For each of the above components of production labor, we calculate the number of hours of work on a yearly basis at each site. (This calculation is complicated by the need to consider learning effects, which are described below.) These hours are then multiplied by a direct labor rate to determine the direct labor cost. Not all components have the same direct rate. Some components are more expensive on a per-hour basis than others. For example, the hourly direct rates for engineering are higher than those for structural mate.

_____

[2]This category includes residual work that must be accomplished post delivery at the FACO location on purchased subassemblies before they can be incorporated into final assembly.

Unit Learning Curve. The number of work hours per aircraft assembled is not static. It has long been understood that manufacturers become more efficient at producing identical items over time. This observation is the "learning effect."[3] We cannot determine the hours worked each year by simply multiplying the production rate by a fixed number of hours per aircraft.

To reflect experience-based gains in efficiency, we use the unit learning curve that represents the production hours per aircraft as a power function of cumulative production. The equation takes the general form:

$$T(n) = T(1) \times n^{\frac{\ln(slope)}{\ln(2)}} . \tag{1}$$

The variable n is the cumulative number of units produced. $T(n)$ is the number of hours for the nth unit. $T(1)$ is the number of hours for the first unit. The variable *slope* is the improvement rate and represents the quantity by which the number of hours gets multiplied each time the production unit number doubles. For example, a slope of 0.95 implies that the unit hours decrease by 5 percent for each doubling of quantity. Therefore, if unit one takes 1.000 hours, unit two takes 0.950 hours and unit four takes 0.903 hours.[4,5]

To determine the number of hours each of the 12 components of FACO labor requires, at a minimum, the calculation of 12 learning curves. However, the RAND model incorporates more complexity. Two additional aspects to production labor for JSF FACO need to be addressed (and were incorporated into the cost model) to reflect the unique nature of this study and of the program: the possibility that

---

[3]Asher, 1956.

[4]The insight that hours required to perform manufacturing functions decline at a set rate as the production units successively double was a foundation of formal cost estimation (Asher, 1956).

[5]It should be noted that Lockheed Martin uses a compound learning curve that changes slope at three points in the production. Its curve mimics an "s"-shaped improvement curve. We have used constant slope curves for our analysis, in line with what the JSF Program Office and the OSD CAIG have done. A comparison analysis using a learning curve like Lockheed Martin's and a simple single slope curve reveals that the difference in labor hours is only about +/– 3 percent. The difference depends on the point at which a second source is introduced.

learning can transfer between sites and the fact that what is being produced is not one single aircraft, but three variants of a single aircraft with a high level of commonality.

Transferable Learning. The efficiency improvement that the unit learning curve reflects results from a combination of factors, including improvements in production methods and experience gained by the workers. All FACO scenarios under examination rely on a single contractor (Lockheed Martin) controlling configuration and methods. Therefore, some, although not all, of the efficiency improvement could plausibly transfer between the various FACO sites. More likely to be transferable are larger-scale engineering improvements or process improvements, including new methods, simplifications of work methods, and tooling improvements. This type of change in the way work is done can be captured in documentation or even shared by engineers traveling between locations. Another kind of learning is generally not so easily transferred—that involved in the work done by touch labor, such as mechanics working on the factory floor. This learning would include start-up or training expertise required for a task, manual dexterity ("learning by doing"), and undocumented tricks or shortcuts that workers might not even be able to articulate.

In the cost model, we have incorporated the flexibility to model learning transfers of different levels between sites. To do so, we split the learning curve for a particular component of labor into two sets of curves, a universal one (for all sites) and a site-specific one. The universal curve is based on the units produced at all sites, whereas the site-specific curves are based on the unit production exclusively at one particular site. The revised learning curve has the form:

$$T(n_i) = T(1)\left\{\gamma n_{all}^{\frac{\ln(slope)}{\ln(2)}} + (1-\gamma)n_i^{\frac{\ln(slope)}{\ln(2)}}\right\}, \quad (2a)$$

where i is an index of location, n_{all} is the cumulative number of units produced at all locations, n_i is the cumulative number of units produced at location i, $T(n_i)$ is the number of hours for unit n_i, and $T(1)$ is the number of hours for the first unit, assumed to be location-independent.

The constant γ is the fraction of learning that is transferable. For example, say a site has produced 23 units of 54 total units. If that site produces the next new unit, n_{all} is 55 and n_i is 24. Note that we assume the universal and site-specific slopes to be identical. We make this assumption because, with the Lockheed Martin management team controlling production, we have no reason to believe that any one site will be able to "learn" more effectively than another, given that the skills required across sites will be the same and that the engineers involved will be able to interact with their counterparts at other sites.[6,7] This implies that formula 2a converges to formula 1 when γ is 1 or one site does all the production (i.e., $n_{all} = n_i$).

The RAND FACO cost model implements equation 2a in a slightly modified form. The unit parameter n for the universal part of the curve is actually the prior year's last unit number (total) plus the site's unit number for the current year. For example, say the prior year's total cumulative production was 57 and that site i had produced 22 of those units. Say this year's total production is 20, of which 10 are produced at site i. For the 10th new unit site i produces this year, n_{all} would be 67 and n_i would be 32. For the first unit produced at site i the next year, n_{all} would be 78 and n_i would be 33. This modification reflects that universal learning would not be transferred instantaneously. We assume a delay of one year for improvements in production efficiencies to be transferred from site to site.

Determining a reasonable value for γ (learning transfer) is problematic. Learning-curve analysis has been typically done at an aggregate level where the cause and effect of the efficiency improvements have not been isolated. Other authors have examined the ability to transfer learning under circumstances where a gap in production occurs.[8] These cases represent an extreme in the transfer of learning. That is, when production is restarted, all of the learning benefit from the workers' efficiency will have disappeared. The efficiency gains from methods improvements should have been cap-

---

[6]This assumes the Northrop Grumman site will be closely tied in with its JSF partner, Lockheed Martin.

[7]To explore how this assumption affects the cost results, we test the sensitivity of one alternative to different learning transfer percentages.

[8]Andelhor, 1969; Birkler et al., 1993.

tured in the processes used to analyze and implement engineering changes. Therefore, a reasonable estimate for the value γ can be determined from an analysis of restarted production. Recasting the data slightly from that reported in Birkler et al. (1993), we find that, on average, 64 percent (percent *Learning Retained* $= \frac{T(1) - T(R)}{T(1) - T(L)}$) of the overall learning (in hours) is retained for production labor, with a range of 30–88 percent. We use this average (and range) as a surrogate for γ (the transferable portion). The remainder of learning will, therefore, be site-specific. The cost model does incorporate flexibility in implementing different assumptions about learning transfer, so further sensitivity analysis on all cases from zero to complete learning transfer can be tested.

Commonality of Variants. The original vision of the JSF program included the cost advantages of having three variants of a single aircraft meet the needs of the Air Force, Navy, and Marine Corps, rather than having each service pay for separate development and production programs. Commonality among the variants is expected to save significant design and production costs (and perhaps maintenance costs for the life of the aircraft). For the production costs specific to FACO, these benefits should also apply.

To represent the effect of the commonality among the three variants, each of the components of labor is determined in the model by a combination of a common and a unique learning curve. We treated "cousin" aspects of commonality as "common" because the assemblies are similar enough to allow for learning transfer among cousin parts.[9] In particular, while cousin parts might have internal differences that affect cost during the fabrication or subassembly process, the interface properties of cousin assemblies and parts are extremely close or identical. Therefore, the shared learning among variants is expected to be high for FACO activities. (The JSF Program Office accepted this approach of treating common and cousin aspects similarly as appropriate for FACO activities.) The formulation of the common and unique learning equation is analogous to equation 2a.

---

[9]Common parts are exactly the same among variants. Unique parts are completely different—the STOVL lift fan is one example. Cousin parts are similar in shape and size but may vary slightly. Thicker spars for increased strength on the CV offer one example.

The equation for one variant (if all production were produced at one site) would be,

$$T_j(n_j) = T_j(1)\left\{\theta_j n_j^{\frac{\ln(slope)}{\ln(2)}} + (1-\theta_j)n_{all}^{\frac{\ln(slope)}{\ln(2)}}\right\}, \qquad (2b)$$

where j is an index of the variant, n_{all} is the cumulative production of all variants, n_j is the cumulative number of variant j units produced, $T_j(n_j)$ is the number of hours for unit n_j, and $T_j(1)$ is the number of hours for the first unit of variant j. θ_j is the work fraction unique for the variant j. We based the values for θ_j on commonality values for the airframe as provided by the Program Office. The percent unique values are 13.3 percent for CTOL, 48.1 percent for CV, and 34.4 percent for STOVL.

Generalizing equations 2a and 2b into a combined formulation, we arrive at

$$T_j(n_{j,i}) = T_j(1)\left\{\begin{array}{l}\theta_j\,\gamma n_{j,all}^{\frac{\ln(slope)}{\ln(2)}} + (1-\theta_j)\,\gamma n_{all,all}^{\frac{\ln(slope)}{\ln(2)}} + \\[2mm] \theta_j(1-\gamma)n_{j,i}^{\frac{\ln(slope)}{\ln(2)}} + (1-\theta_j)(1-\gamma)\,n_{all,i}^{\frac{\ln(slope)}{\ln(2)}}\end{array}\right\}, \qquad (2c)$$

where j is the index of variant and i is the index of location, $n_{all,all}$ is the cumulative number of units produced of all variants at all locations, $n_{j,all}$ is the cumulative number of units produced of variant j at all locations, $n_{all,i}$ is the cumulative number of units produced of all variants at location i, $n_{j,i}$ is the cumulative number of units produced of variant j at location i, $T_j(n_{j,i})$ is the number of hours for unit $n_{j,i}$, and $T_j(1)$ is the number of hours for the first unit of variant j, assumed to be location independent.

Indirect Costs

Indirect costs consist of overhead, G&A expenses, and other components of indirect cost listed later in this report. Overhead costs, the larger of the two, are costs related to fabrication and assembly activities, but cannot be allocated on a direct basis to a particular product for reasons of either practicality or accounting convention. Overhead includes the costs of fringe benefits, indirect labor, depreciation, building maintenance and insurance, computer services, supplies, travel, and so forth.[10] G&A expenses relate more to the company as an entity and may not relate to activity levels at only one plant. The G&A expenses include such general business costs as executive salaries, human resources costs, and the costs of such staff services as legal, accounting, public relations, and financial functions.[11] G&A costs are generally incurred and accounted for at a corporate level, whereas overhead is a site-specific cost.

While these indirect costs are related to and scale with the total direct labor for a site, the relationship is not strictly linear. Indirect costs include both fixed and variable components. As the number of direct labor hours at a site increases, the overhead and G&A rates decrease because the fixed costs are spread over a greater number of hours. To reflect the relationship between direct hours and the indirect cost rates, we use the following formulation:

$$rate_i = \frac{A_i}{\text{Total Hours}} + B_i, \tag{3}$$

where $rate_i$ is the indirect rate, and A_i and B_i are constants. To determine these constants, we surveyed each of the potential sites for their rate information and the sensitivity of those rates to changes in labor base. The constants A_i and B_i for each site were determined by fitting these data (the FY 2001 rate at several hypothesized labor hour levels) to equation 3.[12]

By using the current indirect rate information from each of the sites, we assume that no significant changes to the site or its business structure will occur. This assumption is very tenuous; almost certainly, changes will occur in what each site produces over the next

----

[10]DSMC, 2001.

[11]*Contract Pricing Reference Guides,* Department of Defense Procurement Web site, http://www.acq.osd.mil/dp/cpf/pgv1_0/pgv4/pgv4c2.html (last accessed May 30, 2002).

[12]We are not able to present the results of this analysis because the results are business-sensitive to each of the firms.

few decades. However, it is impossible to predict what these changes might be over the 20-plus years of JSF production, which does not even begin until FY 2006.[13] The potential FACO sites did provide a workload forecast for the next five years.[14] We have assumed a flat workload after the fifth year. This is the best estimate we can make at this time.

The FACO activities for JSF will also change the fixed component of overhead for the sites.[15] For example, some new facilities will be necessary, which will lead to additional depreciation charges, franchise taxes, and property taxes. For the changes to the fixed components of indirect costs caused by FACO, we will calculate each item explicitly and add it to the overhead costs (from equation 3) to determine a new effective overhead rate. This separate accounting was done to isolate the effects of these costs. These explicitly modeled components of overhead (discussed later in this chapter) are

- facilities depreciation
- franchise taxes
- property taxes
- sales and use taxes
- tax credits
- additional power costs
- environmental costs.

Given that increasing the workload at a site typically lowers indirect rates, a benefit accrues to other government programs at JSF FACO sites. The increased workload will decrease the allocated indirect costs for these programs. We calculate the indirect cost savings for these programs as the difference between rates with and without the

---

[13]The 14 SDD aircraft will be built before then.

[14]We have also assumed that all FACO work for a given fiscal year lot is completed in one calendar year. FACO is expected to take only about 40 days, so overlap would be relatively insignificant. However, there is an offset of two years between the fiscal year (year of purchase) and the year that FACO activities complete for the lot.

[15]The formulation of G&A expenses is assumed to be unaffected by FACO activities— that is, the fixed portions of G&A costs do not change when FACO work is added.

FACO activities, multiplied by an average direct wage rate and the number of forecast hours for the other work.

We also include as part of the indirect cost calculations the following:

- fringe benefit costs[16] (e.g., vacation, health insurance, workers' compensation insurance, FICA).
- facilities cost of money (COM).
- overtime premium.
- marketing fees.
- hiring and training costs.

These indirect costs are added based on current Lockheed Martin Aero and Northrop Grumman practices as agreed with the DCMA.

Investments: Facilities, Equipment, and Tooling

To undertake FACO activities for JSF production, a site will need a variety of facilities, equipment, and tooling investments, which were described in Chapter Three. There are two general types of investments:

- **Contractor-owned.** These investments are not specific to the JSF program—i.e., they could be used for other aircraft production programs. An example of such an investment is a paint facility. Contractor-owned facilities, equipment, and tooling are typically subject to property and sales taxes.[17] Cost recovery for these items is through depreciation and cost of money components of overhead.

- **Government-owned.** These investments are specific to JSF FACO activities. An example of a government-owned investment is unique tooling used for JSF FACO work. Government-owned items are not subject to sales and property tax (although some

---

[16]While fringe benefit costs could be considered "direct charges," Lockheed Martin Aero applies a uniform rate to the direct labor dollars for purposes of billing.

[17]As described in Chapter Six, real property (e.g., a building) is not subject to sales tax, regardless of ownership.

states [California, for example] levy a "possessor" tax on such items). The government generally reimburses the contractor in full for these investments.

The investment cost at each site is modeled as a function of the rate of production at the site. For example, the manufacturing floor space required will increase as the annual production rate increases.

We used three steps to determine investment costs:

- **Determine requirement.** Based on the maximum rate that a site will produce over the entire production run, we determine a required level of investment at a site.[18]   Rate dependence is modeled as a step function. For a value between two steps, the requirement is linearly interpolated. The step function can have arbitrary form and can include only one step. For example, a STOVL pad is a requirement for each facility where FACO activities for that variant will take place. One pad is sufficient to handle the highest total annual rate now planned for that variant.

- **Determine facilities/equipment/tooling already available.** Some sites might have existing infrastructure not currently being used and not set aside for other work or programs; therefore, a particular investment might be reduced or not needed at all. This step determines the *usable* facilities, equipment, and tooling existing at a site. This information was obtained though surveys submitted to the sites and through follow-up data collection with the sites.

- **Calculate cost of needed investment.** If the requirement exceeds that already available, the site will need to add an investment. We estimated the cost of such additions based on existing information on such factors such as dollars per square foot, dollars per unit, etc. Lockheed Martin provided most of this investment cost information.

---

[18]The investments have been treated as onetime investments, although, in practice, sites could build up facilities incrementally. However, because the production profile for the JSF builds to a full rate by 2012 and remains rather flat after that, this should not significantly affect the calculations. Also, we assume that assets are not transferred between sites.

Three other variables are tracked along with the investment costs: depreciation, residual asset value, and operations and maintenance costs. Depreciation is tracked because it is an allowable overhead expense for contractor-owned items. Therefore, adding contractor investments to a site will increase the overhead rate through increased depreciation.

Some states have property taxes on manufacturing equipment. Therefore, the residual asset value must be tracked for a new contractor-owned investment to estimate the property tax implications (property tax itself is an allowable cost charged to the government). The residual value for a contractor-owned investment is also tracked to calculate the appropriate facilities cost of money, which is part of overhead. Each year, the residual asset value for these FACO-specific facilities is multiplied by the COM rate to determine the COM charge. We assume the rate to be 5.5 percent.[19]

Some investments might require significant annual maintenance or have significant operating expenses. An example of such an investment would be a thermal oxidizer for pollution control of VOCs. These units require a large amount of natural gas to operate and are expensive to maintain. We assume that the annual level of operations and maintenance cost is a function of the size of the facility or investment.

Table 9.1 summarizes the contractor-owned investments tracked along with the specific depreciation and cost methodology used, as well as the variants whose production requires these assets. Table 9.2 summarizes the government-owned investments. As these items are not depreciated and are general to all variants, depreciation method and variant requirement are not shown.

Taxes and Incentives

Each state has unique accounting rules for taxation that include different tax rates and different definitions of taxable income. For any

---

[19]This is the current (2002) COM rate as published by the U.S. Department of the Treasury. See http://www.publicdebt.treas.gov/opd/opdprmt2.htm (last accessed May 20, 2002).

Table 9.1

Investments Required for FACO (Contractor-Owned)

Item	Cost Factor	Depreciation Type[a]	Variants
Manufacturing space	$/sq ft	Plant/hangars/storage	All
Flight ops run stations	$/unit	Plant/hangars/storage	All
Paint facility building	$/sq ft	Plant/hangars/storage	All
Robotic paint equipment	$/unit	Cranes/other equipment	All
Paint pollution control	$/unit	Cranes/other equipment	All
Storage hangars	$/sq ft	Plant/hangars/storage	All
Administration space	$/sq ft	Plant/hangars/storage	All
Low-observable verification building	$/sq ft	Plant/hangars/storage	All
Low-observable turntable	$/unit	Cranes/other equipment	All
Runway arresting gear	$/unit	Cranes/other equipment	All
Fuel barn	$/sq ft	Plant/hangars/storage	All
270V power transformer	$/unit	Cranes/other equipment	All
Hover pit	$/unit	Cranes/other equipment	STOVL
Hover pad	$/unit	Cranes/other equipment	STOVL

[a]The depreciation rates for these categories come from *IRS Pub 946, Chapter 3*, at http://www.irs.gov. The details are covered in the discussion on facilities.

Table 9.2

Investments Required for FACO (Government-Owned)

Item	Cost Method
Hydraulic test system—Aircraft level	$/unit
Laser trackers	$/unit
Surface finish and appliqué testing	$/unit
General-purpose test equipment	$/unit
Avionics diagnostic equipment	$/unit
Mate alignment tool	$/unit
Dollies and stands	$/unit
Support equipment	$/unit
Maintenance test equipment—Direct	$/unit

two sites in different states, taxes can be quite different, even if the manufacturing operations are identical. To assess the effect of taxes on different FACO strategies, we include in the model four kinds of tax treatments: franchise taxes, property taxes, sales and use taxes, and state and local incentives (which take the form of tax credits and other kinds of benefits—i.e., negative taxation in these cases).[20] These issues were discussed in more detail in Chapter Six.

Franchise taxes are payments to a state for operating a revenue-generating entity in that state. These taxes are analogous to federal corporate income taxes. Determining the state-by-state taxable portion of income for a company that has a presence in multiple states is an intricate process. Most states use an apportionment formula to determine the fraction of the company's total income that is taxable by that state. The formula is based on the fraction of assets, sales, and labor that the company has in the state. Each state being considered in this analysis applies different weights to these components.

To understand fully the franchise tax implications of alternative FACO strategies, we would need detailed financial data for all facilities of the companies involved. Such calculations and data gathering are not practical within the scope of this study and would involve considerable insight and involvement from the contractors' corporate-level tax experts. Therefore, we have taken the following approach to estimating the change in the franchise tax a company would pay if it added FACO activity in any given state. We assume that the additional tax equals the state's corporate income tax rate multiplied by the fee associated with FACO. The state corporate income tax rates were provided in Table 6.1.

This franchise tax simplification has drawbacks. One is that it does not reflect the effect of different states' weighting formulas. Because each state has a different formula, one state might apportion more or less income to itself for identical operations compared with another state. Another, subtler, effect is that companies can use losses from

---

[20]Because this analysis assesses the cost to DoD and not the net cost to the government, we do not include federal income taxes. It should also be noted that federal income taxes are not allowable costs.

other states and even other countries to reduce income in any given state. The apportionment formula is based on *total* corporate income.

Property tax calculations are more straightforward than franchise tax calculations. As discussed above (under "Investments"), the model tracks the residual asset value (original cost minus accumulated depreciation) of FACO property over time.[21] Property taxes are calculated as the product of residual asset value and the property tax rate (see Table 6.1). The reader should note that this calculation is based only on contractor-owned investments, not the tooling and equipment owned by the government. The exception is California, where the contractor is charged a possessor tax for government-owned items.

State sales and use taxes apply to some contractor-owned investments. As described in Chapter Six, some states exempt manufacturing equipment as well as real property from these taxes. We determine a sales tax for each investment, if appropriate, by multiplying the purchase price by the local rate.

Certain states offer tax credits as an incentive to increase local workforces. For every new employee, the company is given a onetime tax credit. For the FACO model, we determine the number of FACO workers based on total number of required work hours divided by the standard hours per year worked. Based on that head count, we calculate the employment credit assuming the number of new hires that will likely be needed by each site, which was provided during the site visits.

States sometimes offer investment tax credits to companies for new plants, facilities, and equipment. These credits are typically a percentage of the total investment cost. Using the investment costs described above, we calculate the investment credit by multiplying it by the credit percentage, where appropriate, and use it to reduce the net franchise tax at site.

---

[21]As a simplification, we have used a common set of depreciation schedules for all sites, based on Internal Revenue Service rules.

Environmental and Permitting Costs

For FACO, the major environmental issues are VOC emissions resulting from painting and finishing activities and noise from flight tests. Environmental and permitting issues can add to overall FACO costs through such requirements as permit fees, preparation and maintenance time, and required equipment and facilities for pollution abatement. These costs are difficult to assess and forecast because few companies typically track them separately as a direct expense by program. Instead, environmental costs are usually part of overhead and are shared among all the work at one site.

Because we had no other method to estimate these costs, we used data provided by the contractor. Equipment needed for FACO-driven environmental reasons is included in the "investment" category. Permit fees are set by the state in Texas and Georgia and by the Air Quality Management District in California. For each location, Lockheed Martin provided an estimate of the permit preparation time and filing fees. For the Palmdale site, these preparation costs are higher because Lockheed Martin anticipates the need to file an EIS. Lockheed Martin also estimated the annual recurring permit costs and fees for each location. These costs have been included in the model.

Noise regulations do not have an associated cost in the model. As discussed in Chapter Seven, noise restrictions may limit or restrict flight-test activities.

Transportation

Typically, the majority (50–70 percent) of the value of any aircraft is produced by subcontractors and then incorporated into the aircraft by the primary assembler. In the case of the JSF, where Lockheed Martin is teaming with Northrop Grumman and BAE Systems, the portion that the prime contractor is contributing is even lower than average. The company estimates that it will have an 18-percent share of the total production value. Hence, much of the material, purchased equipment, and major subassemblies for the production of the JSF aircraft are manufactured at locations other than Fort Worth, and must be shipped to Fort Worth or whichever FACO site is used. Moving the FACO site or adding additional sites will change the cost for shipping these items. The major components that must be available to each FACO site include

- forward fuselage
- center fuselage
- aft fuselage and tail
- wings
- edges
- doors
- weapons bay doors
- engines
- radar.

Changes of FACO location may change transportation costs. For example, Lockheed Martin plans to build many of the components for which it is responsible, such as the wings and forward fuselage, at its Fort Worth facility. If this location is the FACO site, these items will have no transportation costs. For other FACO sites, these items will need to be shipped to the assembly location.

Lockheed Martin plans for truck delivery of all components. For overseas sources, we assume that these items are transported by container ship to a common port—Houston. From that port, the items are trucked to the various FACO sites.

We developed a cost-estimating relationship (CER) to evaluate these trucking costs. We obtained notional quotes to ship partial truckloads of subassemblies from their source (source locations were provided by Lockheed Martin) to the various potential locations.[22] We also determined the driving distance between sites.[23] The CER incorporated into the cost model is

$$\ln(\text{Cost}) = 0.556 + 0.568 \times \ln(\text{Volume}) + 0.392 \times \ln(\text{Distance}), \quad (4)$$

---

[22]Source: http://www.transportation.com.

[23]Source: http://www.mapquest.com.

where,

- Cost is in FY 2002 dollars.
- Volume is in cubic feet.
- Driving distance is in miles.

R^2 was 0.91 with a root mean square error of 0.21.

Crate return costs, if needed, are expressed as a percentage of the initial shipping value.

Power

While electrical power is typically an indirect cost charged through overhead, we have estimated power costs of FACO activities. The estimate has two components. The first is a general facility demand based on square footage of manufacturing space. The power estimate for this purpose is 31.2 kWh per square foot per year, which is independent of the annual production rate (this power is mostly for lighting and heating and air conditioning and, therefore, the power usage is based on facility size). The second component of power cost depends on the annual rate, consisting of the power for high-draw equipment needed for FACO activities. This equipment includes run stations, the fuel facility, the paint facility, and low-observable testing equipment. Each piece of equipment has a power usage per year per station. Each station is assumed to operate at full capacity or not at all. The number of stations assumed to operate in a year depends on the number of JSF aircraft produced. For example, a total of eight paint stations might be at a site, but only six may be used due to workload. At the time this report was written, Lockheed Martin was unable to determine the power usage for each of these facilities. As an approximation, we used the same average power usage per square foot as given above for these items. To arrive at a power cost, the added power demand for the year is multiplied by the site's power rate (dollars per kWh). We assume that the power rates remain stable (in constant dollars) over the production run because it is difficult to forecast future utility prices.

Management and Supplier Support

Having multiple FACO locations will result in additional management, oversight, travel, and communications effort by Lockheed Martin and its suppliers. To estimate these costs, we assume that a fixed number of dedicated prime contractor management representatives will be on site to run the FACO activities at any location outside Fort Worth. The estimate in the model is that 14.0 full-time equivalents (FTEs) would be required for Lockheed Martin representation the first year of production and 7.0 FTEs per year thereafter. The additional 7.0 FTEs for the first year are caused by the setup burden. To arrive at an estimate of the effect of the support costs of management representation on site, the total FTE value was multiplied by an estimated cost of $150,000 per manager (fully burdened).

Having supplier representatives on site to serve their customers is becoming an increasingly common manufacturing practice. We assume that the JSF program will have supplier representatives on site and estimate that 5.0 FTEs are required per year. (The cost of the supplier representatives typically would be included in the price of the component; however, as we do not include the cost of the major subassemblies in our analysis, we treat these costs as a direct cost to the government.)

Fee

The last element to discuss is fee. Fee represents the "profit" earned by the contractor on the cost of the work performed. Typically, the fee is negotiated between the government and the contractor beforehand. To determine a total price, we apply a fixed fee to the direct labor, support labor, and indirect costs. We assume that transportation costs and tooling and equipment costs are passed directly through to the government (i.e., no fee added) with administration expenses associated with those purchases already included in the indirect rates.

MODEL STRUCTURE

Interaction Among Cost Elements

Figure 9.1 illustrates the relationships among the nine cost elements as implemented in the model. Note that we have split investments into two boxes (government-owned and contractor-owned) for ease of presentation.

We now discuss the logic of some of these connections. The site's FACO production plan for a facility will determine the needed investment in facilities, tooling, and equipment (both contractor-owned and government-owned) necessary for the various activities. The greater the rate of production at a site, the more investment will be necessary. These investment costs may be for JSF-specific items (government-owned) and, therefore, are charged directly to the program. Other investments (contractor-owned) get recovered through depreciation charges in overhead. Certain investments might be taxable as property and/or qualify for investment credits—thus the linkage to taxes and benefits. The major investments, such as facilities and equipment, will require power for operation. So, adding

RAND*MR1559-9.1*

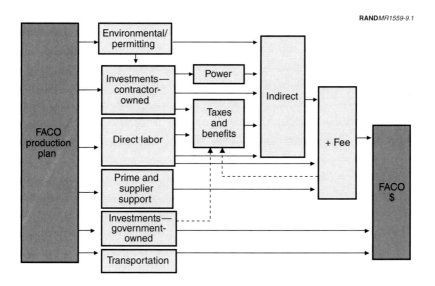

Figure 9.1—Relationships Between FACO Cost Elements

these types of investments increases power costs at the site. Because power costs are included in overhead, the overhead costs further rise with new investment.

Another example is environmental and associated permitting costs. The rate of production will, quite obviously, affect emissions and waste-generation levels and therefore a site's facilities. Environmental and permitting issues also have an additional indirect impact through overhead. Indirect personnel are needed to file and maintain permits as well as to monitor compliance. Furthermore, annual fees associated with a permit must be paid. Finally, some environmental cost is directly coupled with production rate. It may be necessary to purchase environmental "credits" for certain activities (such as painting) as the production rate increases beyond a certain level.

Direct labor for FACO production offers another example. As with the other elements, the direct hours will scale with the production rate at the site. The direct hours for the work will affect the site's overhead and G&A rates. Tax implications exist for the direct hours as well. The fee earned from the labor will count as taxable income for the firm. Another potential effect of the additional workload is to increase employment at the site. If the current workforce cannot accommodate the number of added hours, the firm will need to hire new workers. Also, some states provide tax credits for new hires under certain circumstances. Therefore, increasing workload at a site may result in some additional tax credits as well as additional training costs for the firm.

FACO Production Strategy Assumptions

We made several assumptions about how work would be allocated among multiple sites in this study. We assumed that FACO production would employ a "leader-follower" approach. That is, Lockheed Martin would begin FACO activities of the JSF aircraft at its Fort Worth site (the leader) by producing all of the SDD aircraft there. At some later time, other sites could begin FACO activities for the JSF. This approach is supported by the SDD contract awarded to Lockheed Martin on October 26, 2001, which included no language referring to restrictions on production locations. Lockheed Martin has publicly stated that it intends to do this work at its Fort Worth facility.

(We also have no way to estimate the costs to change the contract so that it includes a requirement to perform FACO at another location.)

The RAND-developed model was flexible enough to analyze the costs of running one to four FACO locations, with any site able to build any percentage of the total production for each JSF variant (0–100 percent). The range of possibilities includes the following:

- Equal percentages of each variant per year per site, so that all sites would perform FACO on equal numbers of variant aircraft over the entire forecast JSF production (subject to minor annual variations because we assume each site would produce a whole number of aircraft each year).

- Allowing one site to perform FACO for all of one or more variants during the entire forecast production, which would lead to different numbers of JSF aircraft being produced by site in some years because of the phasing of the buy quantities by variant.

- Allowing one primary site to build all the aircraft for any length of time in the program, and then having the subsidiary sites split off a portion of the FACO. We assume the decision to split the FACO activities will be made at one time and will hold for the remainder of the program life so there will be no later year-by-year variations in production allocation by site.

Figure 9.2 shows a sample time line for FACO activities. In this example, the primary site performs the FACO activities for all production until a decision is made to establish other FACO locations. After the breakpoint, the primary site continues with the entire CV and some of the CTOL FACO production. Site A does all of the FACO work for the STOVL variant after the break. Site B does the balance of the CTOL FACO work.

CONCLUSION

The cost model contains significant flexibility and incorporates a wide variety of cost elements that would potentially differ among production sites. In the next chapter, we will discuss the specific scenarios we analyzed for different JSF FACO alternatives and the results from the analyses of these scenarios.

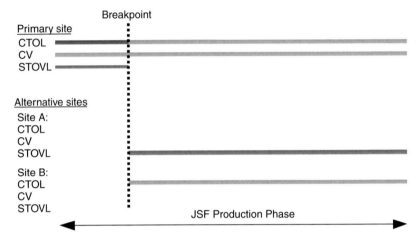

RAND*MR1559-9.2*

Figure 9.2—Example Time Line for FACO Production

Chapter Ten

RESULTS

INTRODUCTION

This chapter presents our estimates of the cost implications of a number of alternative FACO strategies. This analysis employed our model of JSF FACO costs (described in Chapter Nine) to quantify the differences between strategies. The underlying data for the model are based on inputs from contractors, federal and state governments, the JSF Program Office, and RAND's own data. The implications of the alternative strategies are presented as cost differences from the current baseline plan, in which Lockheed Martin performs all JSF FACO activities at its Fort Worth plant. We present the costs of a series of alternatives and test the sensitivities of these results to critical inputs. In no case did DoD save money as a result of any strategy different from the current baseline plan.

COST TO WHOM?

The first step in assessing cost implications is to decide precisely *whose* costs are being included. For this study, we can assess the costs to the following entities:

- U.S. Department of the Treasury/taxpayers
- DoD
- State treasuries
- Contractors

• JSF program.

The total cost to the U.S. Treasury may be the most useful approach from a policy standpoint, but, because of the tremendous complexities in determining taxes for both corporations and individuals that would vary by location, this approach is beyond the capacity of our study to assess. Costs to DoD best reflect the budget implications that a decisionmaker will need to evaluate. For that reason, we view these costs as being the most relevant. Costs to state treasuries or to the contractors are not relevant to the study guidance, so these costs are not assessed. The most straightforward analysis of the strategy alternatives would be to consider the cost effect on the JSF program alone—i.e., to estimate how program costs would change if any or all FACO activities were moved from Fort Worth.

However, determining costs to the JSF program alone ignores the interactions that occur among programs, which affect costs to DoD as a whole. These interactions occur because programs do not take place in isolation. Most weapon system plants have manufacturing work for more than one program at any time. For example, Lockheed Martin's facility in Fort Worth will have ongoing F-16 production work, F-22 mid-fuselage production, and JSF subassembly work, including the forward fuselage and wings. In Marietta, Lockheed Martin builds the C-130J, assembles the F-22 forward fuselage, and performs F-22 FACO. Northrop Grumman performs depot maintenance and modifications on the B-2 and produces the Global Hawk UAV in Palmdale. Lockheed Martin in Palmdale conducts depot maintenance for the U-2 and F-117 and builds parts for the F-22 and the JSF. (This list is not exhaustive.)

These production interactions involve issues of existing and required facilities, availability of workforce, and indirect costs. From a cost perspective, *none* of the work takes place in isolation. For example, costs for required facilities for a new program may vary depending on when other programs shut down and free up existing facilities. Similarly, if workers can move from a program that is in the process of finishing to a new program, hiring and training costs may be minimized. Having other work at the site means that certain indirect costs (for example, plant management) are shared across programs.

Adding a new program to a typical site will reduce the share of indirect costs that other programs must pay at that location, reducing their program costs below what they would have been without the additional work from the new program. Hence, to fully capture costs of doing JSF FACO work at any location, one needs to assess the costs for both the JSF program and other programs at that location. If work is moved from one site to another, the effect on the initial site needs to be assessed and incorporated into total DoD costs. DoD costs are determined by a complex interaction among a variety of factors, including the fixed and variable costs that FACO adds to the overhead (e.g., facilities, power, taxes), the level of other work at the plant, and the sensitivity of the overhead rate to workload.

As discussed in Chapter Five, overhead rate is an example of a rate that is sensitive to workload. The overhead rates at different sites have different sensitivities to changes in workload. If the sensitivity is large, additional work will bring down the overhead rate more than if the sensitivity is small. If a location has a large business base, sensitivity tends to be low, and therefore additional work does not substantially change rates. The rates for a facility with a smaller workload prior to FACO could change more significantly.

To address these complexities, we will present the costs of alternative strategies from the two perspectives of the cost to JSF FACO and the cost to DoD. The total costs to the JSF program as a whole[1] are not calculated specifically, but are included in the net cost to DoD. Thus, the DoD costs incorporate the impact of the alternative strategies on overhead costs for both the JSF and other programs. This approach comes closer to capturing the net cost to the taxpayer. The DoD value is the total effect on all defense programs (including the JSF) at the sites specified in each scenario.

To keep the basic report nonproprietary, total dollar costs for each alternative are not shown; rather, we present the costs as differentials from a baseline case. This approach allows us to present results that do not divulge proprietary data.

---

[1]We do not have sufficient information about the JSF subassembly work to be conducted in Fort Worth to make this assessment.

FACO ALTERNATIVES

Along with the baseline approach of undertaking all of FACO in Fort Worth, many alternative scenarios are possible. These range from giving alternative sites 100 percent of the work to dividing FACO activities across three sites according to some formula. As has been discussed previously, the cost model can assess alternatives including:

- Dividing JSF FACO by some percentage across multiple sites.

- Dividing JSF FACO by variant across multiple sites.

- Varying the point at which the additional sites are added, including adding additional sites at the beginning of LRIP, at the beginning of FRP, or at some other time.

In this chapter, we present the estimated cost implications of the following nine alternatives, which we judge to represent reasonable bounding of the possibilities:

1. 100 percent of FACO at Lockheed Martin–Fort Worth (baseline case).

2. 100 percent of FACO at Lockheed Martin–Palmdale.

3. 100 percent of FACO at Lockheed Martin–Marietta.

4. 100 percent of FACO at Northrop Grumman–Palmdale.

5. 50 percent of FACO at Lockheed Martin–Fort Worth and 50 percent at Lockheed Martin–Palmdale.

6. 50 percent of FACO at Lockheed Martin–Fort Worth and 50 percent at Northrop Grumman–Palmdale.

7. 50 percent of FACO at Lockheed Martin–Fort Worth and 50 percent at Lockheed Martin–Marietta.

8. All CTOL at Lockheed Martin–Fort Worth and all CV and STOVL at Lockheed Martin–Marietta.

9. One-third of all production at each of the three Lockheed Martin sites.

All the alternatives share the following underlying assumptions:

- Lockheed Martin–Fort Worth does all SDD work, regardless of subsequent production-phase FACO work share. The company has already been awarded the SDD contract, which contains no restrictions on site location. Lockheed Martin has stated that it intends to do all the SDD FACO–related work at its Fort Worth site.

- Equipment, tooling, and facilities are not moved between sites. The most costly investments here are the facilities, which would be difficult and expensive to move.

- UK quantities are used for learning-curve and facility requirements, but the cost of the UK aircraft is not included in these results. Because this was a congressionally mandated study, RAND's approach was that the costs to the United States were the appropriate ones to analyze.

- The fee has not yet been determined for the JSF program. Our results are based on an assumed value of 13 percent, in line with historical values for aircraft production programs.

- In cases where 100 percent of the work is transferred to a site other than Fort Worth, the work is assumed to start at LRIP.

- In cases where work on particular variants is split, Fort Worth performs all of the LRIP FACO, and the alternative site(s) start work at the beginning of FRP. (The risks of splitting the initial LRIP aircraft include issues with controlling engineering changes across sites and ensuring that all manufacturing processes are finalized before bringing on additional sites. This approach reduces the risk in the coordination of engineering work across sites.)

- In cases where variants are 100-percent split by site, the work is assumed to start at each site at LRIP.

- Unless otherwise noted, the learning transferred between sites is 64 percent, with a one-year lag. This value represents an average of historical experience with programs that were stopped and subsequently restarted—the best analogy for shared learning.

- Results are in FY 2002 dollars. Undiscounted dollars are presented first, followed by discounted dollars.

Impact of FACO Activities on Site Workload

FACO percentage of total work at the site (including FACO) is presented in Figure 10.1 for alternatives 1–4. The added work varies as a percentage by about 20 percent from the largest effect to the smallest. Even though FACO workload is a relatively small part of the labor hours required per JSF aircraft, placing all the FACO workload at one location has a significant effect on that location's business base. Hence, moving the workload from Fort Worth does not produce a symmetrical change in another location's rates.

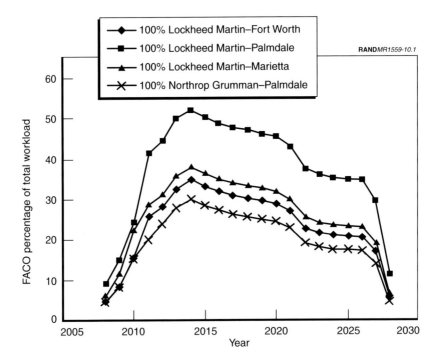

NOTE: Percentage is based on $\dfrac{\text{FACO Workload}}{\text{Base Workload} + \text{FACO Workload}}$.

**Figure 10.1—FACO Workload Share for Alternatives 1–4
(Baseline Activities Without FACO)**

Base Case Versus Alternatives

This section addresses the basic cost questions. Under the alternative JSF FACO scenarios, how much do FACO costs change for the JSF program? How much do total costs change from the total DoD perspective?

Table 10.1 shows the cost differences among the various alternative FACO strategies from these two perspectives. Again, to avoid the possibility that proprietary data can be derived from the results, these costs are presented as differences relative to the baseline, in which all FACO work is done at Fort Worth (i.e., alternative one is defined to have a cost "difference" of zero).

One should not interpret the differences as *necessarily* indicating that one site is more or less expensive or that one producer is more or less costly. Rather, the differences highlight the cost of implementing a strategy other than the baseline approach. This interpretation is particularly true for the reported DoD costs where indirect costs are significant. For a case that shows a net positive (increase) from the baseline, the increased costs could indicate any combination of the following explanations:

- It is more expensive to take work away from the baseline facility when the effect on other programs is considered (effect on overhead rates).

- Inefficiencies in splitting the production make an alternative strategy more expensive (loss of learning).

- A facility/site requires a substantial investment that the baseline site may not require (having invested in some facilities for SDD production).

- Manufacturing costs (e.g., rates for labor, power, management, taxes) are lower at the baseline facility.

- Local environmental regulations are more strict at an alternative location, leading to increased investment and/or recurring costs.

- Additional management and oversight efforts are required to manage an additional manufacturing location that are not required for the baseline facility.

Table 10.1

Cost Differences for Various FACO
Alternatives (millions FY02$)

Alternative	JSF FACO Cost	DoD Cost[a]
1. 100% FACO LM-FW	0.0	0.0
2. 100% FACO LM-P	4.0	256.9
3. 100% FACO LM-M	132.1	74.1
4. 100% FACO NG-P	199.0	656.7
5. 50% FACO LM-FW/50% LM-P	310.3	221.5
6. 50% FACO LM-FW/50% NG-P	328.4	386.4
7. 50% FACO LM-FW/50% LM-M	331.8	117.1
8. 100% CTOL LM-FW/100% CV and STOVL LM-M	419.1	134.7
9. 1/3 production at all three LM sites	501.7	277.6

[a]Includes cost effects from JSF FACO.
NOTE: For full list of alternatives, see p. 152.

Table 10.1 shows that none of the alternatives to performing 100 percent of JSF FACO in Fort Worth saves DoD money. From the program perspective, it is generally less expensive to do 100 percent of the work at any one site.[2] Alternatives involving proportional work shares are usually more expensive. Splitting the work between three sites leads to even higher costs. The factors driving these costs are the additional facilities needed and the loss of learning from splitting production.

The DoD perspective is more complex as the alternatives involving any production in California are the more expensive ones. California's higher costs stem mainly from higher taxes, slightly higher labor rates, more expensive electrical power, and stricter environmental requirements.

---

[2]Some of the likely costs if all JSF FACO work were moved to an alternate site are not captured in the model because these are not FACO-specific costs. For example, there might be some duplication of JSF program managers, and Lockheed Martin might incur the costs of moving managers to the alternative site. These managers are not specifically associated with FACO activities and thus are not included in our model— but this represents a likely additional cost.

Alternatives where Northrop Grumman performs all or part of FACO are more expensive than where Lockheed Martin performs the work. This should not be interpreted as Lockheed Martin being necessarily a more efficient producer than Northrop Grumman. A combination of the reasons listed above interacts to create this effect. It should also be noted that even the most expensive alternative adds less than 10 percent to the cost of FACO, which is only 2 percent of the total JSF URF costs.

To understand the cost differences among the alternatives more fully, it is helpful to examine the contribution of each of the FACO cost components. Tables 10.2 and 10.3 show the contribution of each of the major cost elements for each of the nine alternatives. Table 10.2 shows the cost differences from the perspective of the JSF FACO activity while Table 10.3 shows the cost differences from the DoD perspective. Again, alternative 1 is where 100 percent of JSF FACO work takes place at Fort Worth. Note that the indirect costs and total fees are the only components that change between the JSF FACO and DoD perspectives.

We now discuss the additional fixed indirect costs incurred as a result of FACO activities. Figure 10.2 shows these fixed components of indirect costs for each scenario. Facility costs make up the largest costs. We note that the environmental/permitting category includes only the permitting costs and fees. The cost for emissions-control equipment is included in facilities depreciation and maintenance. We note also that the additional taxes and power costs are higher for California sites.

Sensitivity Analysis

We next test the robustness of these results by relaxing some of the assumptions presented earlier.

Time When Alternative Sources Are Introduced. The point at which the alternative sites start performing FACO activities influences the magnitude of the change in cost. This occurs for two reasons. First, the total loss of learning is reduced if the second site is started later. Second, existing facilities currently used become available as other programs ramp down. (For example, when F-22 production is completed, certain facilities in Marietta will be available for JSF FACO.)

Table 10.2

Contributions to Relative Costs—JSF FACO Perspective (Millions FY02$)

Cost Element	Alternative								
	1	2	3	4	5	6	7	8	9
Direct production	0.0	6.4	1.5	58.2	27.3	48.5	25.2	38.3	38.4
Additional management/ supervision	0.0	22.1	22.1	22.1	16.1	16.1	16.1	20.0	32.3
Indirect/burden	0.0	−33.0	76.7	87.8	199.9	194.8	217.5	282.6	316.6
Transportation	0.0	9.1	18.8	9.1	4.0	4.0	8.1	7.2	7.7
Equipment and tooling (including operations and maintenance)	0.0	0.0	0.0	0.0	19.1	19.1	19.1	10.7	31.8
Supplier and partner support	0.0	0.0	0.0	0.0	10.8	10.8	10.8	14.2	21.6
Fee	0.0	−0.6	13.0	21.8	33.0	35.1	35.0	46.2	53.2
Total	0.0	4.0	132.1	199.0	310.3	328.4	331.8	419.1	501.7

NOTE: For description of alternatives, see p. 152.

Table 10.3

Contributions to Relative Costs—DoD Perspective (Millions FY02$)

Cost Element	Alternative								
	1	2	3	4	5	6	7	8	9
Direct production	0.0	6.4	1.5	58.2	27.3	48.5	25.2	38.3	38.4
Additional management/supervision	0.0	22.1	22.1	22.1	16.1	16.1	16.1	20.0	32.3
Indirect/burden	0.0	190.8	25.4	492.8	121.3	246.1	27.4	30.9	118.3
Transportation	0.0	9.1	18.8	9.1	4.0	4.0	8.1	7.2	7.7
Equipment and tooling (including operations and maintenance)	0.0	0.0	0.0	0.0	19.1	19.1	19.1	10.7	31.8
Supplier and partner support	0.0	0.0	0.0	0.0	10.8	10.8	10.8	14.2	21.6
Fee	0.0	28.5	6.4	74.5	22.8	41.8	10.3	13.4	27.4
Total	0.0	256.9	74.1	656.7	221.5	386.4	117.1	134.7	277.6

NOTE: For description of alternatives, see p. 152.

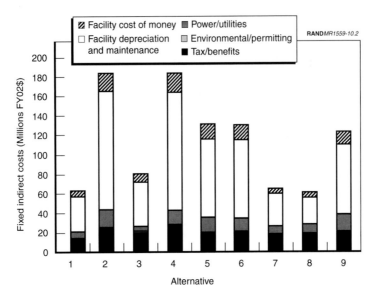

Figure 10.2—Total Additional Fixed Indirect Costs of FACO Activities

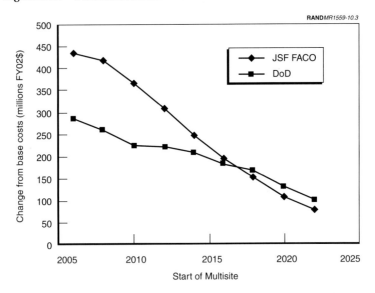

**Figure 10.3—Cost Sensitivity to Change in Start Year of
Multisite FACO for Alternative 5 (50 percent at Fort Worth/
50 percent at Lockheed Martin–Palmdale)**

We assessed the sensitivity of the results of two scenarios (alternatives 5 and 7) to the start date of the split. Figure 10.3 shows the sensitivity for alternative 5.

Figure 10.4 shows the sensitivity for alternative 7. Notice the drop in the DoD curve around 2010. This drop is related to certain F-22 facilities (such as paint booths) that become available around 2012. After 2012, fewer new facilities need to be built to accommodate JSF FACO at Marietta. Also, existing workers will be able to transfer from the F-22 program to the JSF program.

Transfer of Learning. As discussed in Chapter Nine, estimating the exact amount of "learning" transferred between sites is difficult. As a baseline, we have assumed that learning transfer in a work split is analogous to a gap in production. Historically, the fraction of learning recovered following a production gap averages 64 percent (in hours). To explore how this assumption affects the cost results, we

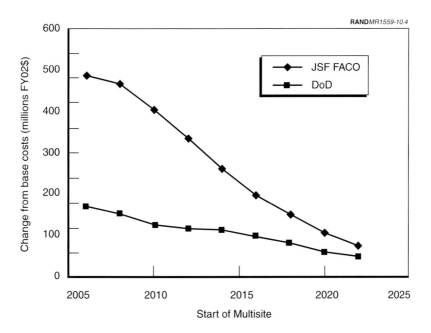

Figure 10.4—Cost Sensitivity to Change in Start Year of Multisite FACO for Alternative 7 (50 percent at Fort Worth/50 percent at Marietta)

tested the sensitivity of alternative 5 to different transfer fractions. (Figure 10.5 shows these sensitivities.) When a higher percentage of learning is transferred, the costs of having a second FACO site decline. However, even at 100-percent learning transfer, the change from the baseline is still positive (higher cost). There are two reasons for this. First, we assumed that a one-year lag occurs in the transfer of learning between sites even if 100 percent is transferred. This incorporates the time lag in communicating lessons between sites. Second, part of the change from baseline costs arises from having redundant facilities at two locations.

Discount Rate. In analyzing the costs and benefits of alternatives with different expenditures and savings over time, the NPV and internal rate of return can be used as metrics. Discounted values weight earlier costs more heavily because money has a time value. We present the cost differences of the alternatives using a discount

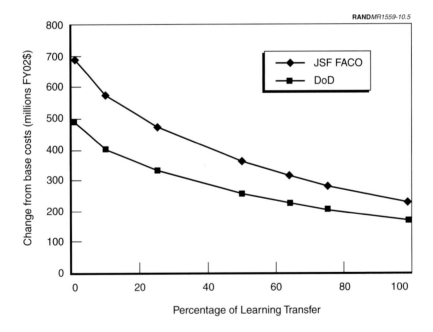

Figure 10.5—Sensitivity to Different Learning Transfer
Fractions of Alternative 5 (50 percent at Fort Worth/
50 percent at Lockheed Martin–Palmdale)

rate of 3.5 percent (the current OMB rate for government analyses having a 25-year duration). These values are shown in Table 10.4.

CONCLUSION

Changing the FACO strategy from the base case of doing all the work in Fort Worth will increase both FACO and total DoD costs. Under every scenario (including those that involve transferring 100 percent of the work to an alternative site), the costs to DoD are estimated to increase by at least $74 million (FY 2002 dollars) from the baseline FACO strategy.

The cases involving work splits are more costly, increasing DoD costs by at least $117 million (FY 2002 dollars). These additional costs are due to loss of learning and extra facilities. The least costly alternative incorporating a work split involves placing part of the FACO work in Marietta, ramping up when the F-22 program finishes. This approach would allow certain F-22 facilities to be reused for the JSF, reducing the total investment required. Also, skilled workers will be able to transfer from the F-22 to the JSF program, reducing hiring and training costs.

However, a downside to this approach is that the JSF FACO work at Marietta would be undertaken essentially in isolation from the rest of

Table 10.4

Relative Cost Increases for Various FACO Alternatives—
Discounted at 3.5 Percent per Annum (millions FY02$)

Alternative	JSF FACO Cost	DoD Cost
1. 100% FACO LM-FW	0.0	0.0
2. 100% FACO LM-P	17.8	180.3
3. 100% FACO LM-M	104.6	61.5
4. 100% FACO NG-P	155.8	446.5
5. 50% FACO LM-FW/50% LM-P	207.4	130.8
6. 50% FACO LM-FW/50% NG-P	219.8	230.5
7. 50% FACO LM-FW/50% LM-M	218.5	75.0
8. 100% CTOL LM-FW/100% CV and STOVL LM-M	302.0	99.5
9. 1/3 production at all three LM sites	333.1	168.9

NOTE: For full list of alternatives, see p. 152.

the JSF program, therefore eliminating the advantages of having collocated production and engineering functions. No other JSF subsystems or parts are being considered for manufacture at Marietta.

Chapter Eleven

CONCLUSIONS

This study found that moving JSF FACO from Lockheed Martin's plant in Fort Worth to one of the other three sites in the analysis or splitting JSF FACO among two or more of these locations would increase costs to DoD. The study assessed other potential policy arguments for moving or splitting production and found no compelling policy arguments to change Lockheed Martin's baseline FACO strategy of doing all the work in Fort Worth.

COST

The previous chapter showed no cost advantages to DoD in moving or splitting JSF FACO activities. All the alternatives that divide the work across one or more additional sites increase cost because of loss of learning and duplicate facilities and tooling. Furthermore, moving FACO activity from Fort Worth changes the overall DoD costs because of the effect on indirect costs for other DoD work. The costs of the rest of the JSF work under way at that plant, as well as of the other programs there, will increase because these programs must bear a greater fraction of the overhead costs. This indirect cost increase is not generally offset by a corresponding decrease for other programs at the alternative FACO sites.

In sum, any alternative that changes the FACO base strategy of doing all the FACO work at Lockheed Martin's Fort Worth plant increases costs to DoD—and to the taxpayer. The least-costly alternative to the base case is shifting part of the FACO work to Lockheed Martin's Marietta plant, enabling the company to use some of the facilities developed for the F-22 fighter to be reused for the JSF, thus reducing total investment. However, a downside to this approach is that the JSF FACO work would be undertaken essentially in isolation from the rest of the JSF program, therefore eliminating the advantages of having collocated production and engineering functions. No other JSF subsystems or parts are being considered for manufacture at Marietta. Because placing JSF FACO at Marietta is not part of Lockheed Martin's planned approach, the effect of these issues is uncertain.

OTHER POLICY ARGUMENTS

Our analysis indicates that some other policy concerns, sometimes raised as a rationale for splitting military production, are not compelling in the case of JSF FACO work. The most-often-cited rationale—spurring better contractor performance through competition—does not apply in the case where a single prime contractor has already been awarded the contract. Some internally generated competition might be possible but could have detrimental effects on configuration control. Neither do other rationales—industrial base, capacity, risk avoidance, etc.—provide compelling arguments for dispersed production. Even the potential advantage from spreading economic benefits across sites does not hold up under close scrutiny. One could also hypothesize that carrying out FACO operations at multiple sites would spread the benefits of the FACO work to several communities. However, three observations lead us to conclude that this argument is not compelling. First, the JSF project is relatively widely dispersed as it is. Figure 2.3 and Table 8.2 provide some indication of the number of communities the program already benefits. Second, the communities that would benefit—Palmdale, Calif., and Marietta, Ga.—are not economically worse off than the country as a whole. In addition, starting FACO operations at another site would not provide an especially large number of new jobs: Direct and indirect labor required for FACO operations is about 1,200 workers. Third, the rationale for the JSF contract—a single contractor building all variants with considerable commonality among them—was to enable DoD to get a needed defense capability at the lowest possible cost. Because moving or splitting FACO operations would increase cost, opting for more than one location appears to undercut the program concept of affordability.

SUMMARY

No compelling policy or cost arguments support a decision to move or divide the FACO operations. Splitting the work would no doubt benefit the communities where the additional sites are located. Whether such a split should occur for this reason, despite the additional taxpayer cost, is not addressed in this study.

LEGISLATIVE LANGUAGE: THE FLOYD D. SPENCE NATIONAL DEFENSE AUTHORIZATION ACT FOR FISCAL YEAR 2001

SEC. 141. STUDY OF FINAL ASSEMBLY AND CHECKOUT ALTERNATIVES FOR THE JOINT STRIKE FIGHTER PROGRAM.

(a) **REPORT REQUIRED.** Not later than 180 days after the date of the award of a contract for engineering and manufacturing development for the Joint Strike Fighter aircraft program, the Secretary of Defense shall submit to Congress a report providing the results of a study of final assembly and checkout alternatives for that aircraft.

(b) **MATTERS TO BE INCLUDED.** The report under subsection (a) shall include the following:

(1) Examination of alternative final assembly and checkout strategies for the program, including—

(A) final assembly and checkout of all aircraft under the program at one location;

(B) final assembly and checkout at dual locations; and

(C) final assembly and checkout at multiple locations.

(2) Identification of each Government and industry facility that is a potential location for such final assembly and checkout.

(3) Identification of the anticipated costs of final assembly and checkout at each facility identified pursuant to paragraph (2), based upon a reasonable profile for the annual procurement of that aircraft once it enters production.

(4) A comparison of the anticipated costs of carrying out such final assembly and checkout at each such location.

(c) **COST COMPARISON.** In identifying costs under subsection (b)(3) and carrying out the cost comparisons required by subsection (b)(4), the Secretary shall include consideration of each of the following factors:

(1) State tax credits.

(2) State and local incentives.

(3) Skilled resident workforce.

(4) Supplier and technical support bases.

(5) Available stealth production facilities.

(6) Environmental standards.

JSF FACO SITE ASSESSMENT

JOINT STRIKE FIGHTER FINAL ASSEMBLY AND CHECKOUT
SITE ASSESSMENT

(To Be Completed by Government Personnel)

Company Name:

City/State/Zip:

CAGE:

DCMA Office:

POC:

Phone:

E-mail:

Section 1. Airfield and General Site Data

a. Provide key dimensions of this site's main runway (length/
    width/overruns).

b. Is this site in compliance with Air Force and Navy safety
    requirements for tactical (Category 5) aircraft (i.e., Airfield, ARFF

Services and Hangar Fire Protection requirements identified in AFMC Instruction 91-101 & NATOPS 00-80-R-14)?   ❑ Yes ❑ No If No, identify deficiencies/waivers.

c.   Briefly describe any planned capital improvements that are expected to significantly improve the capability of this airfield (e.g., a new runway or runway extension).

d.   Are noise or flight path restrictions currently in place that limit the operation of tactical aircraft?   ❑ Yes ❑ No If Yes, identify restrictions.

e.   Do you foresee any airfield encroachment issues that are likely to limit military tactical aircraft operations in the future?

f.   How much land is available for future expansion?

Section 2. Facility Data

a.   **Gross floor space (square feet 000).**

Production (factory)   _____

Administrative (office)   _____

Laboratory   _____

Warehouse   _____

Total Floor Space   _____

b. **Hangar Space.** Provide key attributes of hangars available/ utilized for final assembly of aircraft. Please separate high-bay and low-bay space.

Building #	High-bay/ Low-bay Dimensions (L' × W' × H')	Air Condition- ing/ Humidity Control (Y/N)	Overhead Crane (Y/N) (xx) Ton Capacity	# of Tactical A/C Dock Positions	Current Capacity Utilization (%)

c. **Paint Facilities.** Provide key attributes of hangars available/ utilized to paint complete aircraft.

Building #	Dimensions (L' × W' × H')	Air Condition- ing/ Humidity Control (Y/N)	Robotic or Manual Application	# of Bays/ Positions for Tactical A/C	Air Control Activity?— Active or Passive Filtration

d. **Flight Prep Facilities.** Provide key attributes of hangars available/utilized to prepare aircraft for flight test.

Building #	Dimensions (L' × W' × H')	Air Conditioning/ Humidity Control (Y/N)	Fire Suppression? (Y/N) Type?	# of Bays/ Positions for Tactical A/C

e. **Fuel/De-fuel Operations.** Provide key attributes of fuel operations.

Type (In-ground or Truck)	Use (Fuel, De-fuel, or Both)	Number of Positions	Enclosed (Y/N)

f. **Ramp Space.**

Provide gross square feet of ramp space available at this site.

_____

How many ramp positions are available for tactical aircraft?

_____

g. **Transportation.**

Is the site accessible via interstate highway?   ❏ Yes ❏ No

Is the site accessible via railroad?   ❏ Yes ❏ No

Is the site accessible to Category 6 aircraft (e.g., C-5, 747)?
          ❏ Yes ❏ No

If appropriate, provide additional data on restrictions that may limit transportation access to this site (e.g., unusual weight or height restrictions).

h. **Hush House/Hover Pit.**

Does this site maintain a hush house suitable for engine run-up of tactical aircraft?   ❏ Yes ❏ No
If Yes, provide number and size of enclosure(s) (L' × W' × H').

Does this site maintain a hover pit suitable for VSTOL aircraft testing?   ❏ Yes ❏ No

i. **RCS.**

Does this site maintain facilities and equipment to measure the radar cross section of aircraft components (e.g., leading edges) and/or complete aircraft?

Components   ❏ Yes ❏ No

Complete Aircraft   ❏ Yes ❏ No

j. **Energy.**

What is the current average yearly energy usage (kWh)?_____

What is the average cost per kWh?   _____

Are there back up generators on site that can be used in the case of power outages?   ❏ Yes ❏ No

Have there been any significant outages in the last five years which resulted in a work stoppage?   ❏ Yes ❏ No
If Yes, please describe (e.g., lightning storm, planned or unplanned outage due to electricity generation limitations).

k. **Local Issues.**

What is the general level of public support for this facility? (Check one.)

The community would support a larger presence (e.g., more flight tests).   ❏

The community is neither supportive of nor against the facility.   ❏

There is community pressure to decrease the impact on the local community.   ❏

If there is community pressure, what form does it take (e.g., local organized groups or individuals with concerns about noise, pollution, or other environmental impact)? Please describe.

l.   **Other.**

Does this site maintain the capability to handle and store classified data and equipment?   ❏ Yes ❏ No

Approximately what percentage of the workforce is cleared for
classified material?

Describe any planned capital improvements expected to significantly alter or replace any of the key facilities identified above.

Section 3. Environmental Issues.

a.   Is this facility in a non-attainment area for ozone and particulate
matter (new and old standards)?   ❏ Yes ❏ No

b.   How many air permits exist at this site?   _____

c.   What kind of air control technology exists at this site?
                              ❏ Passive Filtration System
                              ❏ Active Filtration System

d.   What slack (for emissions) is there in existing permits for:

NOx:

VOC:

PM10:

e.   Provide a history of violations, fines paid, and work stoppages for
the last three calendar years.

f.   Describe facilities and permits for handling and storage of hazardous materials (such as paints, solvents, RCS coatings).

g.   Are there storage facilities available on site for limited amounts
of explosives, e.g., ejection seat cartridges?   ❏ Yes ❏ No

Section 4. Historical Data.

a.   FACO will require workers with a variety of skills for production, quality assurance, tooling, general engineering, and indirect labor. Please provide the number of employees in the following key categories. (Note: This table lists categories that are used by some contractors, and is meant to serve as a template. If contractors at your site use different descriptions of skills for production, quality assurance, tooling, general engineering, and indirect labor, provide employee numbers using your contractor's categories.)

	1999	2000	2001	2002
Total Employees				
Touch Labor				
Subassembly operations				
Aircraft final assembly				
Final paint and coatings				
Ramp, flight test, and delivery				
Other Direct Labor				
Quality control				
Manufacturing and sustaining engineering				
Tool manufacturing and engineering				
Indirect Labor				

b.   Number of new production aircraft delivered (by program).

Program	1999	2000	2001	2002

c. Number of Re-delivered aircraft undergoing maintenance and modification (by program).

Program	1999	2000	2001	2002

Section 5. State and Local Government Incentives.

a. Is this site in an Enterprise Zone and eligible for state or local tax and development incentives?   ❏ Yes ❏ No

b. Does the company utilize any **tax exemptions or credits** for state taxes at this site?   ❏ Yes ❏ No
Local taxes?   ❏ Yes ❏ No
If Yes, provide details, including program name.

c. Does the company take advantage of any state business development incentives, such as tax-exempt bond financing, loan guarantees or direct state aid at this site?   ❏ Yes ❏ No
Local incentives?   ❏ Yes ❏ No
If Yes, provide details, including program name.

Section 6. Financial. (The purpose of the following questions is to collect data that will allow for an approximation of the impact or adding or deleting part or all of the JSF final assembly and check-out workload to this facility in the future.)

a. **Wage Rates.** Provide Direct and Indirect Labor and Fringe Rates in the table below.

	1999		2000		2001	
	Labor Rate $	Labor and Fringe Rate $	Labor Rate $	Labor and Fringe Rate $	Labor Rate $	Labor and Fringe Rate $
Production*						
Quality Assurance						
Tooling*						
General* Engineering						
Indirect Production Labor						

*If possible, break these labor rates into the same categories you used for the number of employees in the table of Section 4a.

What are the projections/agreements as to wage increases?

b. Does this site have a Forward Pricing Rate Agreement (FPRA) in place? ❏ Yes ❏ No
If Yes, when was it negotiated? _____
Provide a copy of the latest FPRA or FPRR to the Industrial Analysis Center, P.O. Box 56668, Philadelphia, PA 19111-6668.

Note: If any of the following questions are directly answered in the FPRA (or FPRR), please note that as your response.

c. How far into the future are FPRA rates analyzed and negotiated between DoD and the company at this facility?

d. What is the forecast business base (by program or activity) used to develop the rates for the contractor at this facility? Please list the hours by year for each program. (For programs less than 50K hours, they can be lumped together as an "other" category.)

Program	2001	2002	2003	2004	2005

e. What is the history of the business base at this facility over the last five years in terms of increases or decreases from the current levels?

f. Does the facility have program specific wrap rates? If so, please provide them.   If a composite wrap rate by major function (manufacturing, engineering, QA, etc.) for the entire facility can also be provided, it would significantly aid the study.

g. If there are multiple overhead cost pools at this site, please identify each.   What costs are included in each pool and how these costs are allocated?

h. Do you have models or other methodologies that calculate the impact of additions or reductions of business base on the labor wrap rate at this location?   ❑ Yes ❑ No

i. Provide the following sensitivities of the composite labor wrap rate and overhead rate to changes from the current (FY 2001) business base.

Change in Current Business Base (in hours)	Total Hours	Site Labor Rate Plus Fringe	Overhead Rate	G&A Rate	Total WRAP Rate
+25%					
+10%					
0%					
−10%					
−25%					

j. Please explain how the composite rate is built-up, starting from the basic direct labor through the total WRAP rate. Which costs are treated as direct and which costs are treated as overhead/indirect?

k. What is the facility composite material burden rate by year? What is the base used to calculate the burden rate? Are there different burden rates for contractor-furnished equipment, government-furnished equipment, high-value items versus low-value items? If so, please provide the rates and bases. What would be the impact of an addition of 10%, 25%, and 50% increase in the base? What would be the impact of a reduction of 10%, 25%, and 50% of the base?

l. Does this site share any overhead costs with other locations in the company?   ❏ Yes ❏ No
If Yes, identify other locations.

m. Briefly describe how the G&A rate is allocated across company sites.

n. **Union Representation.** Is the workforce at this site represented by a union?   ❏ Yes ❏ No
If Yes, fill out the table below.

Union Name	Number of Employees	Contract Expiration Date	Last Strike Date

Do union agreements cover multiple company locations? (i.e., Is there a companywide union agreement?).   ❑ Yes ❑ No
If Yes, identify other locations covered.

Appendix C
WAGE COMPARISONS

Table C.1

Wage Comparisons

			Hourly Wage[a]		
FACO Function	SOC Code	Percentage	Fort Worth	Palmdale	Marietta[b]
Structural Mate	51-2011	1.97	$20.37	$22.38	$20.00
Subsystems Mate	51-2011	1.99	$20.37	$22.38	$20.00
Final Assembly	51-2011	15.81	$20.37	$22.38	$20.00
Flight Operations	49-3011	14.01	$20.45	$19.40	$24.69
Manloads/Incomplete Task Logs	49-2094	13.91	$18.92	$20.66	$16.81
Final Coatings	51-9122	13.13	$15.47	$19.85	$15.54
Quality Control	51-2011	17.75	$20.37	$22.38	$20.00
Manufacturing Engineering	17-2112	5.76	$28.74	$30.47	$29.17
Sustaining Engineering	17-2011	2.99	$34.11	$34.74	$34.47
Tool engineering	17-2112	5.51	$28.74	$30.47	$29.17
Tool manufacturing	51-4111	2.85	$22.88	$20.25	$20.16
Material Control	51-2011	4.32	$20.37	$22.38	$20.00
Weighted Average			$20.96	$22.61	$21.10
Percentage Difference from Fort Worth				7.87	0.65

NOTES: The percentages for each final assembly and checkout (FACO) function are based on the *total* hours for production through 2026.

183

Table C.1—continued

[a]Wage rates are the latest values available at state Web sites or the Bureau of Labor Statistics (BLS) Web site. The Marietta wage for sustaining engineering is the average of 1999 and 2000 BLS wages.

[b]Wage data for Standard Occupational Classification (SOC) Code 51-2011 are unavailable for Cobb County or for a larger statistical area, and the BLS wage for Georgia is suspiciously low. This wage is an estimation, based on the average differences of other Fort Worth wages to those in Marietta.

ENVIRONMENTAL REGULATORY PROCESS

The environmental regulatory process is complex. Federal, state, and local environmental departments are largely organized by environmental statutes, most of which are focused on a particular medium—air, water, hazardous materials and waste, etc. Each level of government has differing responsibilities depending on the statute, and states interpret these responsibilities in slightly different ways. Opportunities for public participation differ. States and localities also generate additional requirements and standards. Finally, because each regulated facility has different processes, equipment, and management, the regulatory process will have variable cost and schedule effects.

The costs of environmental compliance may vary among sites for several reasons including standards that differ in terms of breadth and stringency, such as the number of specific substances regulated, allowable emissions levels and standards, and emissions thresholds for regulatory procedures. Another contributor to cost variability may be differing procedures and fees required by the state or locality for obtaining or maintaining permits. These would manifest themselves in corporate costs for administrative activities associated with environmental management, such as engineering analyses, recordkeeping, monitoring, training costs, facilitization expenses, permitting or disposal fees, and emissions fees.

CLEAN AIR ACT

The Clean Air Act of 1970 and the Clean Air Act Amendments of 1990 (CAAA) cover two classes of pollutants: hazardous air pollutants

(HAPs) and criteria pollutants. Standards for each class are established and applied differently. The CAAA identifies 189 HAPs that are subject to technology-based national emissions standards established by industry (called the National Emissions Standards for Hazardous Air Pollutants [NESHAP]). The U.S. Environmental Protection Agency (EPA) was required to establish national air-quality standards (National Ambient Air Quality Standards [NAAQS]) using health-based criteria for the six criteria pollutants: ozone, carbon monoxide, nitrogen oxides, sulfur dioxide, particulate matter (PM), and lead.[1] Stricter national standards for ozone and PM 2.5 have recently been established, and implementation of these standards is under way. Regulatory thresholds and emissions standards vary according to the ambient air quality in the local area. "Nonattainment" areas are areas that do not meet the primary standard. There are five classifications of nonattainment for ground-level ozone (smog)—marginal, moderate, serious, severe, extreme—and two for carbon monoxide and particulate matter—moderate and severe. The Marietta and Fort Worth Lockheed Martin sites are in serious nonattainment areas for ozone; the Palmdale sites are in a severe nonattainment area for ozone; and the Marietta and Fort Worth sites are in attainment for the other five criteria pollutants. The EPA has not determined whether the Antelope Valley Air Quality Management District (AVAQMD) is in attainment for particulate matter.

The states mainly administer the national standards established in the CAAA. The primary mechanism used to control criteria pollutants is the permit. State-to-state permitting rules and procedures vary, but, in general, a permit allows a facility to release a given amount of the pollutant. Emissions thresholds for determining a stationary source's permitting status are determined by the type of pollutant and the local air quality. As air quality worsens, controls become required for smaller sources. Permissible emissions levels are determined by the desired ambient air-quality standards, the attainment status of the region, and available emissions credits. Moreover, if a given facility wants to release more of a criteria air

---

[1]Volatile organic compounds (VOCs) are not listed as a criteria air pollutant, but, because they are a precursor for ground-level ozone and particulate matter, they are included in efforts to control ground-level ozone. In addition, many are considered HAPs.

pollutant than specified in an existing permit, an offset (a reduction greater than or equal to the increase) must be obtained elsewhere, either at the facility or at other sources in the region, before a new permit may be issued. New and modified sources are subject to review by the state or local air district. These sources may be subject to stricter standards depending on the local air quality.

For the HAPs, NESHAPs are established for each source category of these pollutants—for example, there are national emissions standards for aerospace manufacturing and rework.[2] NESHAPs for engine-test facilities are currently under development. Sources defined as major sources—those emitting 10 tons per year of any one of the listed toxins or 25 tons per year of a combination of toxins—are required to abide by the EPA standards. The standards identify the compliance options (HAP content, control devices, etc.) required to limit pollutant releases.

Air Emissions

The Clean Air Act stipulates that federal actions will not

- Cause or contribute to any new violation of any NAAQS in any area;

- Increase the frequency or severity of any existing violation of any NAAQS in any area; or

- Delay timely attainment of any NAAQS or any required interim emissions reductions or other milestones in any area.[3]

If the site cannot comply with the CAAA, the action cannot be pursued because of the air conformity rule and, therefore, the CAAA legislation is mandatory for the site. Texas and Georgia have Title V permitting authority, and the Lockheed Martin facilities in Marietta and Fort Worth are both well below the thresholds of established air emissions standards. Thus, it is unlikely that if an Environmental

---

[2]Examples include HAP and VOC maximum allowable content in coatings or control device efficiencies used during painting.

[3]The material in this section is distilled from Resource Applications, Inc., 1995; and Bowers and Ling, 2000.

Impact Statement (EIS) were performed at either location, this National Environmental Policy Act (NEPA) process would lead to *additional* emissions controls. In Palmdale, Lockheed Martin will likely obtain enough emissions offsets, either by drawing on its current stock of emissions credits or by purchasing additional credits to satisfy conformity requirements.

Noise

Noise is regulated by local ordinances, not state or federal regulations. Ordinances typically limit allowable noise levels by location for given times of the day. Therefore, there is no direct cost impact, although operational restrictions could translate into cost. More than likely flight test will occur during the day, although at high-rate production, it is possible that delivery, especially for overseas customers, might optimally be performed at night. Noise is also a community-relations issue. Because we are analyzing sites where aircraft manufacturing is established, the noise issue is not likely to make a difference, although it is considered in the analysis. Responses to a Defense Contracting Management Agency site survey indicate that noise is not likely to be an issue at either of the three sites of interest. According to the survey responses, no flight path restrictions are in place for tactical aircraft and no encroachment concerns are anticipated.

NATIONAL ENVIRONMENTAL POLICY ACT

NEPA is federal legislation that requires environmental impacts be considered in any federal program or action before initiating such action. The law is referred to as a "procedural" law because it does not require certain *outcomes* of the decisionmaking process, but rather it prescribes the *process* required for federal decisionmaking. It also includes provisions for public notification and involvement in the decisionmaking process.

NEPA applies to federal actions and programs. For example, they are routinely performed for new weapon system basing decisions and base realignment decisions. In the case of JSF FACO, both government-owned, contractor-operated plants and contractor-owned, contractor-operated plants could conceivably fall under

NEPA. The Fort Worth site (AFP 4) and Marietta site (AFP 6) are government-owned and contractor-operated and the Palmdale site has pieces that are government-owned and contractor-operated (Sites 2 and 7 on AFP 42) and pieces that are contractor-owned and contractor-operated (Plant 10). The NEPA legislation lays out three possible paths for considering the environmental effects of federal actions. The particular path taken depends on the magnitude of the proposed action, current activities at the site, and community response.

Legal experts in DoD have interpreted the NEPA legislation to exclude contractor-owned, contractor-operated plants because private entities are responsible for making these manufacturing location decisions (moreover, program environmental analyses are already performed as part of the acquisition process).

As a result of NEPA, and depending on the specific circumstances, either of the following three paths could be taken (in order of increased expense, time, and analysis detail).

- *Categorical exclusion.* A categorical exclusion is a determination that the proposed action will not have a significant environmental impact on existing conditions at the site.

- *Environmental Assessment (EA).* An EA is an analysis to determine whether the proposed action has either minimal or significant environmental impact.

- *Environmental Impact Statement.* EIS is a complete and thorough evaluation of all the environmental effects that a proposed action may have and includes options to mitigate these effects.

Our analysis, based on discussions with numerous experts in DoD and on a cursory review of available historical data, indicates that the most likely course of action that will be taken at all government-owned, contractor-operated locations, assuming no new construction is involved, is to obtain a categorical exclusion, which does not have associated cost or schedule implications (described below). Should new construction be required, an environmental analysis, with the finding of no significant impact, is likely to occur. Only under extremely unusual circumstances should a comprehensive EIS be necessary.[4]

STATE ENVIRONMENTAL PROTECTION ACTS

Some states have their own NEPA or processes resembling NEPA as well. For example, both California and Washington State require state and local agencies to perform environmental impact analyses when granting permits. Georgia and Texas do not have state-level environmental protection acts.

Activities at the Palmdale site therefore would be subject to the California Environmental Quality Act (CEQA). The act applies to projects performed by state and local government agencies. Issuing environmental permits is considered a project under this act. Permit applicants typically pay for the analysis. An initial assessment determines a project's significance, and the three possible findings are negative declaration for no significant impacts, mitigated negative declaration if there are significant impacts but the project is revised to mitigate these impacts, and environmental impact report if there are significant impacts. Permitting by the AVAQMD does not trigger a CEQA review because permitting is not considered a "project" as defined by CEQA.[5] The FACO process could conceivably trigger CEQA review of the conditional use permit, however, by the city of Palmdale or by Los Angeles County.

---

[4]Personal interviews with Jean Hawkins, JSF/JPO Deputy Environmental Team Leader, April–December 2001; Harry Knudsen, ANG/CEV, August 2001; Jack Bush, Air Force ILE, August 2001; and Lt Chad Schroeder, JSF/JPO Environmental Team Member, September 2001; personal communication with Alison Ling, OASN/I&E, September 2001. See also *Navy Commanding Officer's Guide to Environmental Compliance*, Naval Facilities Engineering Center, Office of the Chief of Naval Operations, September 1995; *OPNAVINST 5090.1B*, Chapter 2, "Procedures for Implementing the National Environmental Policy Act" (NEPA), September 9, 1999; *A Guide to Understanding NEPA*, USAF, accessed via http://www.denix.osd.mil/denix/Public/News/AF/NEPA/ nepa.html, September 2001; AFI 32-7061, January 24, 1995; and Memorandum from AFMC LO/JAV to ASC/YFMM entitled "National Environmental Policy Act (NEPA) Requirements for Weapon Systems Production Activities at GOCO Plants," dated September 24, 1999.

[5]Personal communications, Alan DeSalvio, air-quality engineer, AVAQMD, February 2002.

California has set its own ambient air-quality standards, and they are stricter than the federal standards. The EPA has not classified AVAQMD's attainment status for particulate matter, but the AVAQMD is a nonattainment area under state standards. California's ozone standard is more stringent than the federal one. This stricter standard, however, imposes no additional regulatory requirements (at least for now) than those required by the EPA.

BIBLIOGRAPHY

Aerospace Industries Association (AIA), *Meeting with DUSD(ES) on December 17, 1996,* cited in the Advanced Amphibious Assault Vehicle Program Office submission to the Secretary of Defense Environmental Security Awards for Pollution Prevention in Weapon System Acquisition, April 1997, p. 4.

Andelhor, George, "What Production Breaks Cost," *Industrial Engineering,* September 1969.

Asher, Howard, *Cost-Quantity Relationships in the Airframe Industry,* Santa Monica, Calif.: RAND, R-291, 1956.

Bartik, Timothy J., *Who Benefits from State and Local Economic Development Policies?* Kalamazoo, Mich.: W.E. Upjohn Institute for Employment Research, 1991.

Birkler, John L., Joseph P. Large, Giles K. Smith, and Fred S. Timson, *Reconstituting a Production Capability: Past Experience, Restart Criteria and Suggested Policies,* Santa Monica, Calif.: RAND, MR-273, 1993.

Birkler, John L., and Joseph P. Large, *Dual-Source Procurement in the Tomahawk Program,* Santa Monica, Calif.: RAND, R-3867-DR&E, 1990.

Birkler, John L., Edmund Dews, and Joseph P. Large, *Issues Associated with Second-Source Procurement Decisions,* Santa Monica, Calif.: RAND, R-3996-RC, 1990.

Birkler, John L., John C. Graser, Mark V. Arena, Cynthia R. Cook, Gordon Lee, Mark Lorell, Giles Smith, Fred Timson, Obaid Younossi, and John G. Grossman, *Assessing Competitive Strategies for the Joint Strike Fighter*, Santa Monica, Calif.: RAND, MR-1362-OSD/JSF, 2001.

Bowers, Terry, and Alison Ling, *Information Paper: CAA General Conformity Rule*, CNO N457E/Navy OGC, February 15, 2000.

Brennan, Geoffrey, and James M. Buchanan, *The Power to Tax: Analytical Foundations of a Fiscal Constitution*, New York: Cambridge University Press, 1980.

Bureau of Labor Statistics Web site at www.bls.gov.

_____, 1999 employment at http://stats.bls.gov/oes/1999/oes_11Ma. htm (last accessed May 30, 2002).

_____, employment projections at http://www.bls.gov/emp/ emptab21.htm (last accessed May 30, 2002).

California Energy Commission, *2002–2012 Electricity Outlook Report*, staff draft report, P700-01-004, November 2001.

_____, *2002–2012 Electricity Outlook Report*, commission final report, P700-00-004F, February 2002.

CCH State Tax Handbook, Chicago: CCH Inc., 2000.

Cho, Aileen (with Tom Ichniowski, Andrew Roe, William J. Angelo, and Paul Rosta), "Runway Building Legislation Lingers but Airport Work Soldiers on," *Engineering News-Record*, Vol. 247, No. 10, September 3, 2001, p. 20.

City of Fort Worth, *Strategy 2000: Diversifying Fort Worth's Future*, Economic Development Office, at http://www.fortworthgov.org/ cmo/econdevelop/index_econdevl.asp (last accessed May 30, 2002).

_____, *State of the City and Long Range Financial Forecast: FY 2000–2001 to FY 2004–2005*, at http://www.fortworthgov.org/cmo/ budget/lrff0105/lrff1.pdf (last accessed May 30, 2002).

City of Palmdale and the California Trade and Commerce Agency, *JSF Site Cost-Effectiveness Study*, June 17, 1999.

City of Palmdale, Economic Development Department, *Growth Factors*, Winter 2000.

Cook, Cynthia R., and John C. Graser, *Military Airframe Acquisition Costs: The Effects of Lean Manufacturing*, Santa Monica, Calif.: RAND, MR-1325, 2001.

The Council of State Governments, *State Business Incentives: Trends and Options for the Future*, 2nd edition, Lexington, Ky., 2000.

Darce, Keith, "Ship Swap Deal in Work: Defense Contracts May Go to Avondale," *New Orleans Times Picayune*, January 29, 2002, p. 1.

Defense Acquisition Deskbook Web site at http://web2.deskbook.osd.mil/default.asp (last accessed May 30, 2002).

Defense Systems Management College (DSMC), *Indirect-Cost Management Guide: Navigating the Sea of Overhead*, Defense Systems Management College Press: Fort Belvoir, Va. (2001 update), at http://www.dsmc.dsm.mil/pubs/gdbks/icmguide.htm (last accessed May 30, 2002).

Drewes, Robert W., *The Air Force and the Great Engine War*, Washington, D.C.: National Defense University Press, 1987.

EER Systems, *Environmental, Safety and Health Cost Analysis Guide*, El Segundo, Calif., prepared for Air Force Materiel Command, May 22, 1998.

Environmental News Service, "US Ecology Closes Ward Valley Office," December 9, 1998.

Federal occupational data at http://stats.bls.gov/oes/oes_ques.htm (last accessed May 30, 2002).

Gholz, Eugene, and Harvey M. Sapolsky, "Restructuring the U.S. Defense Industry," *International Security*, Vol. 24, No. 3, Winter 1999/2000, pp. 5–51.

Gray, Wayne, *Manufacturing Plant Location: Does State Pollution Regulation Matter?* National Bureau of Economic Research, Working Paper 5880, January 1997.

Joint Strike Fighter contract award at http://www.defenselink.mil/news/Oct2001/b10262001_bt543-01.html (last accessed May 30, 2002).

Joint Strike Fighter Program Office, *Joint Initial Requirements Document III*, February 7, 1998.

Kearns, Sean, "Plant 42 Underground Wells Contaminated," *Antelope Valley Press*, December 7, 1998.

Latham, Andrew, "Conflict and Competition over the NATO Defence Industrial Base: The Case of the European Fighter Aircraft," in David G. Haglund, ed., *The Defence Industrial Base and the West*, London: Routledge, 1989.

Levinson, Arik, *An Industry Adjusted Index of State Environmental Compliance Costs*, National Bureau of Economic Research, Working Paper 7297, August 1999.

LM Aero Review of the California Proposal Regarding the JSF Program, May 2, 2001.

Mayo, Elton, *The Social Problems of an Industrial Civilization*, Boston: Harvard Business School Press, 1945.

Mineta, Secretary Norman Y., Speech to the U.S. Chamber of Commerce, Washington D.C., February 2, 2001, at http://www.dot.gov/affairs/020201sp.htm (last accessed May 30, 2002).

National Crosswalk Service Center Web site at www.state.ia.us/ncdc.

National Imagery and Mapping Agency (NIMA), *IFR—Supplement: United States* (Effective December 27, 2001, through February 21, 2002), St. Louis, Mo.: NIMA, 2001.

Naval Air Warfare Center, Aircraft Division Lakehurst, Cost Analysis Branch 4.2.5, *Environmental Life Cycle Cost (ELCC) Model: Final Report/User's Manual*, Version 1.2, March 2001.

"Navy, GD and Northrop Cement Long-Planned Swap of Shipbuilding," *Inside the Navy*, June 24, 2002.

Noble, George P., III, *Environmental Practices in Program Office Management*, Fort Belvoir, Va.: DSMC Press, TR 1-95, January 1995.

Oates, Wallace E., *Fiscal Federalism*, New York: Harcourt Brace Jovanovich, 1972.

_____, "Environmental Federalism in the United States: Principles, Problems, and Prospects," National Center for Environmental Decision-Making Research working draft, January 1998. Available at http://www.ncedr.org/pdf/oatespap.pdf (last accessed May 30, 2002).

Reilly, Clint, "Task Force Silent on Jet Noise," *The Virginian-Pilot*, July 8, 2001.

Resource Applications, Inc., *US Air Force Conformity Guide*, Falls Church, Va., August 1995.

Rich, Michael D., William L. Stanley, John L. Birkler, and Mary E. Vaiana, *Cost and Schedule Implications of Multinational Coproduction*, Santa Monica, Calif.: RAND, P-6998, 1984.

Rich, Michael D., William L. Stanley, John L. Birkler, and Michael Hesse, *Multinational Coproduction of Military Aerospace Systems*, Santa Monica, Calif.: RAND, R-2861, 1981.

Roethlisberger, F. J., and William J. Dickson, *Management and the Worker*, Cambridge, Mass.: Harvard University Press, 1939.

Salomon, Roy, and Orjan Sterner, *Environmental Considerations in the Systems Acquisition Process*, U.S. Department of Defense and Armed Forces of the Kingdom of Sweden, Washington, D.C., 1999.

Sampogna, Mike, "New Chamber Chief Sees Brighter Economy," *Marietta Daily Journal*, January 10, 2002.

SDS International, "JSF Site Cost-Effectiveness Study," Arlington, Va., 1999.

Sell, Nancy, *Industrial Pollution Control: Issues and Techniques*, 2nd edition, New York: John Wiley & Sons, 1992.

"Shipbuilding Giants May Swap LPD-17 and DDG-51 Work Worth Billions," *Inside the Navy*, January 28, 2002.

State of California legislation at http://www.usc.edu/dept/ engineering/efc/issues/pdf/ab_60_bill_19990721_chaptered.pdf (last accessed May 30, 2002).

State of California wage data at http://www.calmis.cahwnet.gov (last accessed May 30, 2002).

_____, "CONCEPT PAPER: Proposed Consistent Administrative Enforcement Authority Under the Unified Program," Department of Toxic and Substance Control, California Environmental Protection Agency, July 27, 2001.

_____, "Cal/EPA Environmental Management System Project, Report to the Legislature: Seventh Quarterly Update October Through May 2001," at http://www.calepa.ca.gov/EMS/Publications/2001/ 7thQtr/Introduction.htm (last accessed May 30, 2002).

_____, California Air Resources Board, Enforcement Program, at http://www.arb.ca.gov/enf/enf.htm (last accessed May 30, 2002).

State of Georgia, wage data Web page at www.dol.state.ga.us.

_____, *Rules for Air Quality Control*, 391-3-1-.02(2).

_____, Department of Industry Trade and Tourism, *A Georgia Summary*, October 2001.

_____, Department of Natural Resources, *Rules for Air Quality Control*, Chapter 391-3-1-.03(1)(a)-(c).

State of Texas, Administrative Code.

_____, Smart Job Web site at www.tded.state.tx.us/smartjobs.

_____, Department of Economic Development, "Doing Business in Texas," revised August 1, 2001.

_____, wage data at http://www.twc.state.tx.us/customers/rpm/ rpmsub3.html (last accessed May 30, 2002).

Sterngold, James, "City Known for Military Jets Is Beyond Them," *New York Times,* October 19, 2001, p. A14.

Sweetman, Bill, "How LO Can You Go?" *Jane's International Defense Review,* January, 2002, pp. 20–47.

Sweetman, Bill, and Nick Cook, "Hidden Agenda: What Next for 'Low Observables' Technology?" *Jane's Defence Weekly,* Vol. 35, No. 25, June 20, 2001, pp. 58–73.

Tersine, Richard J., *Principles of Inventory and Materials Management,* New York: Elsevier Science, 1988.

Tompkins, James A., "Facilities Size, Location, and Layout," in Gavriel Salvendy, ed., *Handbook of Industrial Engineering: Technology and Operations Management,* New York: John Wiley & Sons, 2001, pp. 1465–1501.

U.S. Department of the Air Force, *Air Force Instruction 32-7061,* January 24, 1995.

_____, memorandum from AFMC LO/JAV to ASC/YFMM entitled "National Environmental Policy Act (NEPA) Requirements for Weapon Systems Production Activities at GOCO Plants," September 24, 1999.

_____, *A Guide to Understanding the National Environmental Policy Act,* accessed via www.denix.osd.mil, September 2001.

U.S. Department of Defense, *Contract Pricing Reference Guides,* Volume 4, *Advanced Issues in Contract Pricing,* Chapter 2 "Evaluating Indirect Costs," Department of Defense Procurement Web site at http://www.acq.osd.mil/dp/cpf/pgv1_0/pgv4/pgv4c2.html (last accessed May 30, 2002).

U.S. Department of Energy, *Energy Information Administration State Electricity Profiles,* 2001a.

_____, *Annual Energy Outlook 2002 with Projections to 2020,* DOE/EIA-0383(2002), 2001b.

_____, *Energy Information Electric Power Monthly,* 2001c.

U.S. Department of the Navy, *Navy Commanding Officer's Guide to Environmental Compliance*, Naval Facilities Engineering Center, Office of the Chief of Naval Operations, September 1995.

_____, *OPNAVINST 5090.1B*, Chapter 2: "Procedures for Implementing the National Environmental Policy Act," September 9, 1999.

U.S. Department of Transportation, *Airport/Facility Directory* (all regions, effective July 12–September 6, 2001), Silver Spring, Md.: National Aeronautical Charting Office, 2001.

U.S. Environmental Protection Agency (EPA), EPA Office of Compliance Sector Notebook: Profile of the Aerospace Industry, Office of Enforcement and Compliance Assurance, Washington, D.C., November 1998.

U.S. General Accounting Office (GAO), *Environmental Protection: More Consistency Needed Among EPA Regions in Approach to Enforcement*, Report to the Chairman, Committee on Small Business, U.S. Senate, GAO/RCED-00-108, June 2000.

Whittle, Richard, "JSF Would Save Lockheed Jobs," *Dallas Morning News*, August 23, 2001, p. D1.

Williams, G. Chambers, III, "Airports Across the Country, Including Dallas/Fort Worth in Texas, Are Almost Ready for the January 1st Federal Noise Standards to Come Into Effect," *Fort Worth Star-Telegram*, September 20, 1999, p. 1.

Wilson, John D., "A Theory of Interregional Tax Competition," *Journal of Urban Economics*, Vol. 19, 1986, pp. 296–315.

Zahn, Brenda, "Plant 42 Chromium Levels Near State Limit," *Antelope Valley Press*, December 15, 2000.

Zodrow, George R., and Peter Mieszkowski, "Pigou, Tiebout, Property Taxation, and the Underprovision of Local Public Goods," *Journal of Urban Economics*, 1986.